Larry W. Glasser

LOVING · THE · CHURCH

October 2015

Great Book!

Falling in love with the church is a much-needed message for Hispanic leaders everywhere. I am thrilled that New Church Specialties is committed to servicing Hispanic church leaders with their teaching. Together we must speak a language of love.

Dr. Jesse Miranda, National Hispanic Leader
President, AMEN Ministries

What has deeply impressed me about New Church Specialties is the way the training they offer to church leaders is saturated with God's Word. Not only is the training practical and principle-driven, it is always delivered in a spirit that encourages personal, spiritual renewal. You will find Larry McKain's writing filled with clear, practical strategies that are totally immersed in Scripture.

Dr. Keith Wright, District Superintendent
Kansas City District Church of the Nazarene

At a time when many have given up on the church, Larry McKain takes us back to square one—loving the church as Christ does. In this book, he refreshes our love for and devotion to the church. If enough catch this love, we will experience a revival all across North America.

Dr. Aubrey Malphurs, Professor, Dallas Seminary
President, The Malphurs Group

It is enormously refreshing to hear someone stand up for the powerful, positive role interdependence plays among Christians and local churches. Larry McKain demonstrates that kind of courage and insight. He speaks with integrity as one whose personal journey has involved moving past the reality of organizational flaws and overcoming interpersonal hurts. His love affair with the Bride of Christ is an example of seasoned discipleship.

Dr. Jerry Pence
General Director of Evangelism and Church Growth
The Wesleyan Church World Headquarters

Having attended a New Church University training event, I experienced firsthand Larry McKain's passion for the church and its mission in the world. In reading this book, I discovered the same passion and focus. The emphasis on loving the church, warts and all, is a corrective to the overzealous individualism of our era. This is a must-read.

Bishop David G. Mullen, Sierra Pacific Synod
Evangelical Lutheran Church of America

Passion for the church is in short supply these days. Many are short on loyalty and love. Martin Luther seconds Larry's motion and emotion when he reverberates, "God is my Father and the Church is my mother." Reading this book causes me to remember the joy that I first felt when I became a part of the Body of Christ.

Dr. Barry K. Carpenter
Kentucky Conference of the United Methodist Church

Larry McKain's passion for seeing people come to faith in Christ is contagious. It is especially refreshing that he begins his discussion with a theology of the church. His love for the church shines through in all he writes. Dr. McKain challenges the church not only to fulfill its call to mission but also to be the people of God in healthy and holy relationships. *Loving the Church* is a timely book that pastors and church leaders will find to be full of insight and practical instruction.

Dr. Ron Benefiel, President
Nazarene Theological Seminary

If you work in the church and care about the church, read this book. Larry McKain eloquently makes the case for falling in love with the church—or falling in love with the church again. If you have been hurt, disappointed, or disillusioned by your experiences, then you must read this book and find new hope for God's only plan to save the world.

Marcus Bigelow, President
Stadia New Church Strategies

Every pastor, young or old, will be greatly helped by reading *Loving the Church* by Larry McKain. Larry makes the case both for belonging to the church and for connectedness as well as I have ever read or heard. It is worthy of required reading for church membership!

Dr. Bill M. Sullivan
Retired Evangelism and Church Growth Director
Church of the Nazarene

Dr. Larry McKain brings to life the biblical relationships between Jesus, His followers, and His church. Jesus, who loved the church and gave himself up for the church, is our model. A life spent loving the church as Jesus loved the church will be a life well invested—a life of great influence. This book will be of great benefit to all who read it.

Bishop Roger Haskins, for the Board of Bishops
Free Methodist Church

I want to recommend Larry McKain's book *Loving the Church*. I heard Larry give a presentation on this subject, and it so impacted me that I brought him in to Grove City Church of the Nazarene just to bless our congregation. Larry is right on target about what the church world needs to hear today. Everyone will benefit from reading this book.

Dr. Bob Huffaker, Pastor/Church Consultant
Grove City, Ohio

In 30 years of church planting, I have not seen anyone with Larry McKain's passion for Christ's church at large. He possesses a powerful command presence, yet without arrogance. Giving help to churches, NCS has arisen out of Larry's personal passion for the church. If we practice the message of this book, it will lead us to personal and church renewal.

Phil Spry, Founder of Tellstart and Church Plant Strategies
Clayton, North Carolina

[handwritten inscription:] Larry W Glasser
September 26, 2005

LOVING · THE · CHURCH

Connecting to Your Community of Faith

LARRY McKAIN

Beacon Hill Press of Kansas City
Kansas City, Missouri

Copyright 2005
by Larry McKain and Beacon Hill Press of Kansas City

ISBN 083-412-193X

Printed in the
United States of America

Cover Design: Brandon R. Hill

Library of Congress Cataloging-in-Publication Data

McKain, Larry, 1956-
    Loving the church : connecting to your community of faith / Larry McKain.
        p. cm.
    Includes bibliographical references.
    ISBN 0-8341-2193-X (hardcover)
    1. Church. I. Title.

    BV600 .3.M355 2005
    262—dc22

                                                            2005012617

10   9   8   7   6   5   4   3   2   1

I dedicate this book to laypersons, sacrificial and faithful people who unselfishly give themselves week by week for the vision of Christ's church. God knows each of you by name (Exod. 33:17) and "He will not forget your work and the love you have shown him as you have helped his people and continue to help them" (Heb. 6:10).

CONTENTS

ACKNOWLEDGMENTS

Every time I take a moment and reflect on the journey the Lord has all of us on, I am reminded that ministry is fully the result of the dozens of mentors God has given me along the way. The list includes my parents, Marvin and Jo McKain, who modeled love for the church in their everyday lifestyle; pastors I knew growing up like Dr. Crawford Howe; college and seminary professors like Dr. Larry Fine, Dr. Chic Shaver, Dr. Mendall Taylor, and Dr. Ralph Earle; denominational supervisors like Dr. Forrest Whitlatch, Dr. Reeford Chaney, Dr. Charles Thompson, and Dr. Keith Wright, who gave me opportunities to serve God's church, as well as exhibiting "great patience and careful instruction" (2 Tim. 4:2) as they supervised me. It also includes great churchmen God used like Dr. Raymond Hurn, Dr. Paul Cunningham, and Dr. Bill Sullivan, who all modeled before me great commitment to Christ's church.

Some of my mentors were laypeople, men and women in local churches, too numerous to mention, but the lessons they taught were priceless. Some mentors came by way of books and tapes, people like Rick Warren, Bill Hybels, John Maxwell, Max Lucado, and others. In the early 1990s, Bob Logan built and delivered the first Church Planter's Toolkit and coaching resources, which helped me grow. Another exceedingly great mentor is John Wesley, whose life has influenced me greatly. He has passed on, but through his writings, "by faith he still speaks" (Heb. 11:4).

Words also cannot describe the joy I feel in being able to work with the tremendous New Church Specialties team God has brought together—our Board of Directors, Marvin McKain (an incredible chief financial officer who serves so capably for $1 a year); senior staff: Lonnie Bullock, Scott Chamberlain, and Phil Stevenson; senior consultants: Dr. Dan Croy,

Dr. Bob Huffaker, and Joe Knight; NCS support staff: Karen Bullock, Darla Elliott, Denise McKain, Connie Vandersteen, and a host of other part-time staff who serve as coaches, help with NCU, and so forth. As I reflect on the adventure we are on together, my heart is full for the privilege of locking arms in ministry with each of you.

Finally, a huge debt of gratitude goes to my wife, Denise. It has been her love, faithfulness, and unselfish support these past 25 years that has made the journey a wonderful joy. I love you, Denise. Thank you for your heart of compassion for the poor and less fortunate, your giving spirit, and everything you do every day for God, the church, and our family.

INTRODUCTION—
GOD IS AT WORK!

*"So I prophesied as he commanded me, and breath entered them;
they came to life and stood up on their feet—
a vast army" (Ezek. 37:10).*

In our day, I hear the sounds of a new army coming! The sounds are not that of a congregation that continues to "do church" as they have always done before. The sounds I hear are the marching of those who hear the beat of a different drum. They are the innovators, the risk-takers, the ones who are anxious for adventure. They know they are called, spiritually gifted, and led by God. They include both clergy and laypeople. They are a growing group of new people within a new movement. They are a new army of people in NewStart, ReStart, ReFocusing, and Parent churches who see the church in a whole new way.

The leaders in this new army are different from the ordinary. In many ways, they are a breed apart. They do not come a dime a dozen, but they are a growing group of people critical to the long-term health and multiplication of Christ's church. They have a certain mix of spiritual gifts that God has uniquely endowed them with, in order to multiply the entry points into the kingdom of Christ[1] through planting, refocusing, parenting, and creating the climate where "God movements" can happen.

Discontented with status quo and ordinary church routine, they feel the same urge as was felt in the heart of the apostle Paul. "It has always been my ambition to preach the gospel where Christ was not known, so that I would not be building on someone else's foundation" (Rom. 15:20). When planting, refocusing, or parenting a church, the same motivation as the apostle Paul is present—to reach people who do not know Christ.

♦ ♦ ♦

There is a new army God is raising up in NewStart, ReStart, ReFocusing, and Parent churches.

♦ ♦ ♦

Another characteristic of this new army is that they understand their work often goes unnoticed. When the gospel made its greatest advance in the Book of Acts, non-Jews (men from Cyprus and Cyrene) went to Antioch and spoke to Greeks about Jesus (Acts 11:20). We have all heard about Paul and Barnabas being sent as the first church planting leaders from Antioch (13:2-3). Antioch was the first parent church in the New Testament and launched the church planting movement of the Christian faith. But have you ever considered who started the Antioch church? From the Bible, we do not even know their names. But we do know "the Lord's hand was with them, and a great number of people [in Antioch] believed," so Jerusalem headquarters sent Barnabas down to find out what was going on (11:21; see v. 22).

Where "God movements" happen, there are always scores of unnamed people working behind the scenes. They get little credit or recognition for their labor. But when they get to heaven, they will hear our Savior say, "Well done, good and faithful servant!" (Matt. 25:21). For them, that is enough because their ultimate purpose in life is to bring glory to God, not themselves.

♦ ♦ ♦

The ultimate purpose of life and the church is to bring glory to God.

♦ ♦ ♦

Whether we are speaking one-on-one or reading a book by someone, after we spend time with a person and understand his or her thinking, we discover the person's attitudes, spirit, and heart. Paul instructs us, "So . . . whatever you do, do it all for the glory of God" (1 Cor. 10:31). God created everything to reflect His glory. "The heavens declare the glory of God; the skies proclaim the work of his hands" (Ps. 19:1). Any person who lives for his or her own glory, sins. Paul wrote, "for all have sinned and fall short of the glory of God" (Rom. 3:23).

Seeking our own glory rather than God's glory so easily happens, even in God's church. It occurs when our desire to be noticed or recognized becomes stronger than our passion to bring glory to God. We are kept "from willful sins . . . blameless [and] innocent" (Ps. 19:13) when we "fan into flame" (2 Tim. 1:6) our passion for God alone to be glorified.

Jesus' great desire was to bring glory to God. The night before Jesus died, He prayed to His Father, "I have brought you glory on earth by completing the work you gave me to do" (John 17:4). Paul thunders this focus when he writes, "Now to him who is able to do immeasurably more than all we ask or imagine, . . . to him be glory in the church and in Christ Jesus throughout all generations, for ever and ever! Amen" (Eph. 3:20-21). In our work in God's church, we must remember it is *all* about God, not us. The ultimate purpose of life and the church is to bring glory to God!

This is a book designed for laypeople. Its purpose is to help us better understand what God thinks about the church and how we should think about it too. We will use five words that may be new to you, so let me define what we mean.

NewStart: the start of a new church

ReStart: the start of a new church with the use of a former building and/or remnant group of people

ReFocusing: the process of recapturing the vision and heart of Jesus for His church to be radiant, healthy, and multiplying. This requires moving the church from an "inward" to an "outward" focus.

Parenting: taking personal ownership of a NewStart or ReStart project to multiply the Kingdom. It may involve one church or a group of churches coming together.

Judicatory: a generic term used to describe the organizational structures in various denominations (i.e., conferences, districts, synods, presbyteries, conventions, dioceses, associations, regions, etc.). While church polity differs among denominational families, all denominations are made up of a collection of judicatories.

Church health and church multiplication are a high priority for numerous judicatories and denominations across North America. Numerous books on church health strategy and structure have been written. A large number of programs highlighting starting new churches, restarting churches, refocusing local congregations, and parenting new churches have now been developed. These are new church "specialties that have emerged as the church continues to find better ways of achieving God's mission in the world."

Every sincere layperson I meet wants to be a part of a healthy church. What we need to understand are the attitudes toward the church we must have if this is to be achieved. I have learned that everything begins with how a person thinks and what they collectively believe about the church. Many North American Christians operate with a biblically fuzzy understanding of the church. Many do not love the church as Jesus loves it. We contend that if your church is to be the kind of congregation you have always dreamed about being part of, it begins with you having a clear understanding of the nature of the church.

God is glorified and His mission in the world advances greatly when groups of Christians lock arms together in His name to do the work of expanding His church. When God's church enjoys unity and agenda harmony, she is unstoppable! David writes, "How very good and pleasant it is when kindred live together in unity" (Ps. 133:1, NRSV). "For there the LORD bestows his blessing, even life forevermore" (v. 3). A key issue related to building a healthy church is gaining agenda harmony. What is agenda harmony? Let me define what we mean by these two words.

Agenda: "an outline or plan of the things that must be done"

Harmony: "a unified arrangement of parts with a common focus"

◆ ◆ ◆

God's mission begins with my local church,
but it is much bigger than that.
What is at stake is the salvation of our planet.

◆ ◆ ◆

Put together, agenda harmony occurs when the members of a local congregation and judicatory work together for a common objective, with a common purpose, in a common spirit.

The apostle Paul knew the importance of agenda harmony within the church and wrote, "If you have . . . any fellowship with the Spirit, . . . then make my joy complete by being like-minded, having the same love, being one in spirit and purpose" (Phil. 2:1-2). How good and pleasant it is when a local church and judicatory has these four characteristics: (1) they are like-minded; (2) they have the same love; (3) they are one in spirit; and (4) they are one in purpose.

We contend that this is not just a suggestion or an option to God. The Lord can bestow His blessing, even everlasting life (see Ps. 133:3), *only* where there is unity and agenda harmony. Only where people are one in spirit and have the same love will we see lost and broken people come to Christ. It is only as local churches and judicatories are "brought to complete unity to let the world know" (John 17:23) Christ's church as He designed us to be. We do not contend for structural unity but for spiritual unity.[2]

For the sake of the church Jesus loves, we urge every Christian to "make every effort to keep the unity of the Spirit through the bond of peace" (Eph. 4:3). Unity of the Spirit does not mean I operate in practical independence and have an attitude of doing my own thing. The health and mission of God's church begin with my own local church. But at the same time, *it is much bigger than my local church.* What is at stake is the salvation of our planet. This is not just about ourselves. God says a combination of unity and agenda harmony is the *only way* a spiritual climate is created that will consistently lead numbers of people to faith and eternal life. Having a healthy church requires agenda harmony among both the local congregation and the judicatory with which it is connected.

I desire the following four ideas to shape the spirit of this book about the church: (1) God is at work raising up a new army of laypeople who love their church. (2) Much of their work goes unnoticed. (3) Their ultimate purpose is to bring glory to God. (4) Agenda harmony is required for God's blessings on a local church and the judicatory they are part of.

A healthy church is never the result unless the people within the church are able to gain agenda harmony. Gaining biblical agenda harmony is where many churches fail. Great agenda harmony is gained by using and applying Scripture. It is gained through the work of the Holy Spirit who creates and sustains the church. It requires people to have a clear spiritual understanding of the church. Spiritual power and spiritual results come through the Holy Spirit and the use of Scripture. It is Scripture that softens people's hearts, builds agenda harmony, and brings transformation in people's lives.

This book has been written to help you better understand what you should believe about the church. What we believe greatly impacts how we behave. My prayer is that after you read *Loving the Church* you will learn to see and love the church as Jesus does. He literally "gave himself up for her" (Eph. 5:25). He expects us to do the same. Our desire is that God will take these pages and use them for the health and multiplication of His church, until the earth is "filled with the knowledge of the glory of the LORD, as the waters cover the sea" (Hab. 2:14) and "the kingdom of the world has become the kingdom of our Lord and of his Christ, and he will reign for ever and ever" (Rev. 11:15). Our prayers are with you.

1
CHANGING THE · WAY WE · THINK

"Christ loved the church and gave himself up for her to make her holy, cleansing her by the washing with water through the word, and to present her to himself as a radiant church, without stain or wrinkle or any other blemish, but holy and blameless" (Eph. 5:25-27).

I AM THE FIRST TO SEE HER WHEN she appears . . . she snaps heads sideward with every row she passes. That's the way it is with the bride. She remains hidden from friends and relatives . . . until the playing of the four-measure fanfare of Wagner's Wedding March. Then the notes of the fanfare sound. She steps out in view of all of us . . . Row by row, people turn to face the center aisle. They gasp, they cry, they laugh, they beam, they rejoice. The bride stands us on our heads. She is the center of the wedding and radiates every hope and dream on that day. Maybe that's why God chose the symbol of the Bride to represent the church. Christ meant for His church to turn heads.[3]

◆ ◆ ◆

We must begin with the biblical and very practical issue of loving the church, even when she is imperfect.

◆ ◆ ◆

We have all been to weddings. The first miracle that Jesus performed was at a wedding (John 2:1-11). In the Old Testament, God refers to the people of Israel as His Bride (Hos. 2:19-20). In the New Testament, Paul likens the nature of the church to the marriage of a husband and wife: "the two will become one flesh. This is a profound mystery—but I am talking about Christ and the church" (Eph. 5:31-32). In the final book of the Bible, John describes the greatest wedding of all time taking place at the Marriage Supper of the Lamb (Rev. 19:6-9). The church is the Bride of Christ and will belong to Him for all eternity.

Paul Dramatically Changed His Attitude

Kevin Meyers is a NewStart church planter in Hilliard, Ohio. I will never forget how my heart burned as Jesus used him to open the following scriptures to me (Luke 24:32). They deal with the biblical and very practical issue of loving the church even when she is imperfect. Following the death of Stephen and before the conversion of Saul, persecution was great against the church. "All except the apostles were scattered throughout Judea and Samaria" (Acts 8:1). The Bible says that "Saul began to destroy the church. Going from house to house, he dragged off men and women and put them in prison" (v. 3). But on the road to Damascus, all that changed when Saul had a divine moment with God. A light from heaven flashed and a voice spoke, "Saul, Saul, why do you persecute me? . . . I am Jesus, whom you are persecuting" (9:4-5).

◆ ◆ ◆

Any wrong I do to the church,
in God's eyes I do to Jesus.

◆ ◆ ◆

Do you see the inescapable link? The Bible says that Saul was persecuting *the church* (8:3). He was trying to destroy *the church*. But in Acts 9 Jesus makes clear that Saul is not just persecuting an imperfect group of people. When he speaks badly of, when he hurts with his words or actions, when his attitudes toward the church are wrong, he hears a voice say, "I am Jesus, whom you are persecuting." The teaching of the Bible here is clear. Any wrong I do to the church, in God's eyes I do to Jesus. This same persecutor later writes, "This is a profound mystery, but Christ and His church have become one flesh" (see Eph. 5:30-31). What an attitude change he had! When he really met Jesus, Paul dramatically changed his attitude toward the church.

◆ ◆ ◆

**When he really met Jesus,
Paul dramatically changed his attitude
toward the church.**

◆ ◆ ◆

As a layperson, you have no doubt heard stories about people who do not want to become committed Christians because of their criticism of Christ's church. Just as Paul did before he was converted, thousands of people have persecuted Jesus in ignorance when they have intentionally done things or held attitudes that harm Christ's church. From the Cross where He hung and died for their congregation, we can still hear Jesus whisper, "Father, forgive them, for they do not know what they are doing" (Luke 23:34). There are millions of people in North America today who say they love Jesus; however, they cannot accept the imperfect people who make up the church. This is a book that, in part, has been written to deal with this heresy.

I wish I could report to you that this all-pervasive attitude of apathy and criticism toward the church is only found outside God's family. But sad to say, it is not. As I have traveled across North America, I have found that many people within the church have the same incorrect attitudes as the people outside God's family have. They love Jesus, but at best they tolerate the church. In their thinking, because of its imperfections, it is too much of a spiritual stretch for them to love it.

◆ ◆ ◆

**Many people within the church love Jesus,
but at best they tolerate the church.**

◆ ◆ ◆

As a Christian, I do not have the luxury of deciding the attitudes I will or will not keep. When I read something in the Word of God that challenges my attitudes or thinking, I cannot ignore it. I am not given the option of rationalizing my attitudes away by looking at someone else and saying, "I may not be perfect, but I sure am a lot better than him or her." Christlikeness is the standard by which we are all measured. Jesus left us "an example, that [we] should follow in his steps" (1 Pet. 2:21).

There is no teaching more important for a healthy church than a correct, biblical, and practical understanding of the church. We have studied Willow Creek, Saddleback, and numerous other churches where the Holy Spirit is at work transforming people's lives. All of these churches differ greatly in church polity, theological beliefs, strategy, and structure. But they all have one thing in common. They are filled with people who love the church and are giving themselves up for her. They are following the example of Jesus when it comes to their attitude and practical belief about His church. God has given us clear teaching in His Word. These God-inspired ideas from Holy Scripture should deeply affect the way you and I think about the church.

The Huge Impact of Our Thinking

How we think makes a big difference. It makes all the difference in the world and in the world to come. How we think is not as much what we say but what we are. What we ultimately become is determined by how we think. There is a little saying that clearly describes how we become what we are.

♦ ♦ ♦

What we ultimately become is determined by how we think. This is true of local churches, judicatories, and even entire denominations.

♦ ♦ ♦

Sow a thought, reap an act.
Sow an act, reap a habit.
Sow a habit, reap a character.
Sow a character, reap a destiny.

How we think leads to how we act. How we act determines the habits we form. The habits we form determine the character we possess. Our character determines our destiny. This is true not only of individuals but also of local churches. This is true of judicatories and even entire denominations.

How we think makes a *huge* difference. In our local church or judicatory, we are all a product of how we think. If the wonderful church you and I are part of is to be all that God has dreamed for her to be, it will begin with us and the way we think. If you and I are to be used in our generation to help the church be what Jesus gave himself up for her to be, we must learn to think the way Jesus thinks. We must see lost people the way Jesus sees lost people (Luke 15:1-32). We must act the way Jesus would act, if He were the church in our skin. Because He is. We are His body, His flesh in the world today (1 Cor. 12:27). As His church, we are given the incredible promise that it is possible for us to have "the mind of Christ" (2:16).

Agenda Harmony with Jesus

♦ ♦ ♦

Never underestimate the power of God-inspired thoughts and ideas.

♦ ♦ ♦

Jesus was the greatest leader who ever lived. His coming to earth cut our calendar in two. Every time you and I write a check, we are reminded of how many years it has been since God entered the bloodstream of humanity. Jesus changed the world with shared thoughts and inspired ideas. Through the power of the Holy Spirit, the movement of Christianity erupted—and that movement has impacted your life. Jesus had a vision for His church. He gave himself up for her and what she could be. He changed the world with teaching— with thoughts and ideas that came from God. He said, "For I did not speak of my own accord, but the Father who sent me commanded me what to say and how to say it" (John 12:49).

♦ ♦ ♦

I want to think the way Jesus thinks, feel what He feels, and cry over what He cries over. I want my will to be guided by His will and my values to reflect His values.

♦ ♦ ♦

Never underestimate the power of God-inspired thoughts and ideas. This is why the teaching and preaching that occurs in your church every week has so much potential! God uses it to literally transform people's lives. Jesus died for your church. He carries it in His heart and mind. He says to you, "I know your deeds, your love and faith, your service and perseverance" (Rev. 2:19). He has called you and me to join with Him as He builds His church (Matt. 16:18). To be more effective, we must learn better how to speak beyond our own ideas. We must have a deeper sense that the Father is telling us both what to say and how to say it to the church we love and serve. We must always choose our words with care (James 3:1-2).

You will notice in this book we use a lot of scripture. This is because large parts of this book have come from both prayer and insights from God's Word. Remember, great agenda harmony is gained through the work of the Holy Spirit and by using and applying scripture. In my own life, when I hit a wall or face personal obstacles that cause me to change, a key shift usually occurs when I change my way of thinking because of the impact of scripture. Positive change starts happening when I begin seeking agenda harmony with Jesus.

The more I mature in the Lord and seek to follow His agenda, the more often I find myself asking questions like, "What does Jesus think about this?" "How does He feel?" "What would Jesus do?" I find myself praying prayers like, "Lord, help me to cry over the things that make You cry, to laugh at the things that make You laugh, to have a heart for the things for which You have a heart." I want to think the way Jesus thinks, feel what He feels, and cry over what He cries over. I want my will to be guided by His will and my values to reflect His values. I want my spirit to be filled with His Spirit and my heart to be aligned with His heart. I want to learn how to think the way Jesus thinks. I want His agenda to be my agenda.

This kind of thinking shift has led me to the Bible. I wish I could tell you every decision I make these days consistently lives up to the ideals in the paragraph above. It does not, but my heart is there. Over time I feel that my mind is slowly being renewed. More and more I am less driven by what Larry thinks and more consistently guided by what Jesus thinks. Gaining agenda harmony with Jesus is a process. Paul describes it this way: "Do not conform any longer to the pattern of this world, but be transformed by the renewing of your mind. Then you will be able to test and approve what God's will is—his good, pleasing and perfect will" (Rom. 12:2).

◆ ◆ ◆

If your heart is responsive, a "God movement" has already begun where you live.

◆ ◆ ◆

If the church we serve is to change for the better, it will always begin with you and me changing the way we think as Christians. It will require us letting God regularly renew our minds by His Word so that we will gain His agenda and come into harmony with the other Christians with whom we serve. The result we seek is to lock arms together and create the vision Jesus has for His church, being "like-minded, having the same love, being one in spirit and purpose" (Phil. 2:2). Do you have any interest in being part of a church like that? If your heart is responsive, a "God movement" has already begun where you live.

2
WHAT · WE THINK · ABOUT · THE CHURCH

"At the center . . . Christ rules the church. The church, you see, is not peripheral to the world; the world is peripheral to the church"
(Eph. 1:22, TM).

OVER THE PAST SEVERAL YEARS, I have traveled hundreds of thousands of miles speaking to hundreds of churches. I love them all—rural and urban, large and small, rich and poor, highly educated or with just lots of common folks. In the whole world, there is nothing else quite like the church. What a marvelous creation of God! What an incredible design! What a divine strategy! God takes imperfect people all over the world who believe in Jesus, and He gathers them into divine groups. These groups meet every week for prayer, teaching, encouragement, and correction from His Word. They lock arms with each other to provide a witness to the world that they are one with Jesus and the Father (John 17:21-23).

♦ ♦ ♦

The church—what a marvelous creation of God! What an incredible design! What a divine strategy!

♦ ♦ ♦

If you are a typical Christian living in North America, you probably love Jesus a lot more than you love His church. One of the reasons I feel compelled to write this book is to help you recover a correct, practical doctrine of ecclesiology. As a layperson, don't let the word *ecclesiology* scare you away. Let's break it down. *Ology* at the end of a word simply means "the study of." Let's look at a couple of examples. Take the word *theology*. The Greek word for God is *theos*. So theology is "the study of God." Take the word *salvation*. The Greek word for salvation is *soterios*. So soteriology is "the study of salvation."

Now take the word *church*. The Greek word for church is *ecclesia*, which literally means "the called out ones" or "the assembled." We are called out of the world, assembling ourselves together (Heb. 10:25) and regularly being changed by God's Word to be sent back into the world. Ecclesiology is the study of the church. The study of Christ (Christology) and the study of the church (ecclesiology) are so interlocked that no Christian can be a true follower of Christ without the church.[4]

The sad truth is that literally millions of Christians have spent their entire lives attending church, serving within the church, and relating to the church, but they have never gone through a biblical study of the church. They have not learned nor have they been taught the attitudes they should have toward the church. They do not have a good, practical doctrine of the church. Paul instructs us, "Watch your life and doctrine closely. Persevere in them, because if you do, you will save both yourself and your hearers" (1 Tim. 4:16).

♦ ♦ ♦

Millions of Christians have not learned nor
have they been taught the attitudes they
should have toward the church.

♦ ♦ ♦

In many Christian circles, the word *doctrine* has come to be a negative thing. Doctrine is thought of as "dogma," something that is rigid, that causes me to disagree with other Christians, that creates opportunities for intellectual debate. This was never the understanding of the apostle Paul. Doctrine was much more practical, because for him, doctrine was directly tied to a person's behavior. He warns young Timothy, "Watch your life and doctrine closely" because he knew that both of these would affect the behavior of the church dramatically.

How God Changes Our Behavior

♦ ♦ ♦

A change in behavior always flows
out of a change in beliefs.

♦ ♦ ♦

Do you have anyone in your church whose behavior needs to change? Do you have anyone whose attitude or actions need adjusting? If you are like me, sometimes the adjusting needs to be in me! So what do we do? We must begin with one basic premise—a change in behavior always flows out of a change in beliefs. People behave because of what they believe. How do we get people to believe differently? We do not. That is the Holy Spirit's job. We cannot change other people's beliefs. But we can change our own beliefs, and we do need to better understand how the Holy Spirit changes both us and the people around us.

♦ ♦ ♦

A divine moment is a spiritual step of obedience
a person takes, in response to the
Holy Spirit's prompting.

♦ ♦ ♦

He regularly uses some spiritual resources or "spiritual tools." In one place Paul describes them literally as spiritual weapons. He writes, "The weapons we fight with are not the weapons of the world. On the contrary, they have divine power to demolish strongholds" (2 Cor. 10:4). There are some people and some churches that try to operate with worldly resources; they try to change people without spiritual tools, and the result is always harm and loss.

Paul seems to see a spiritual battle taking place between the forces of God and the forces of evil, *even in the lives of very good people like you and me.* Every time personal transformation takes place, a change of mind occurs! It almost always happens, not just in giant leaps but in little steps. It is the Holy Spirit at work. We call these spiritual steps divine moments, or "God moments." It is not something we do; it is something God alone does. As a Christian, have you ever thought about the resources, the tools God uses to change you? Have you ever reflected on how God changes the people around you?

Divine Moments Create a Healthy Church

In building "a church so expansive with energy that not even the gates of hell will be able to keep it out" (Matt. 16:18, TM), the New Testament teaches us that there are several spiritual resources God uses. Let me mention at least five: (1) prayer, (2) the Word of God, (3) the Holy Spirit,* (4) an individual believer living a life of integrity, and (5) the collective witness of the church. At times, one weapon or tool by itself does not seem enough to help me win the spiritual growth battle. But when all the weapons in God's arsenal are used together, Satan's work is tied up and his influence is driven back (Matt. 12:29). God can and does use multiple spiritual re-

---

*Although the Holy Spirit is God, the third person of the Trinity, and quite unlike any of the other resources listed, He is included among them because He is powerfullly at work creating divine moments in people's lives.

sources as He creates divine moments that cause spiritual growth in my life.

You may be thinking, "Can you more fully explain what you mean by 'divine moment'?" A divine moment is a spiritual step of obedience I take, in response to the Holy Spirit's prompting. It always involves me somewhere along the process of moving from where I am, to becoming a "global disciple." My decision to begin attending church, my decision to accept Christ, a decision for baptism, becoming a self-feeding Christian, joining a Sunday School class or small group, me desiring spiritual growth and accountability, my decision to join the church, my becoming a worshiper, my experience and growth in sanctification, my getting involved in the church, me using my spiritual gifts in meaningful ministry, my decision to become a tither, my decision to give beyond the tithe to the mission of Christianity worldwide, my decision to engage in personal witnessing—all of these are steps along this process.

♦ ♦ ♦

God uses the church to help people take spiritual steps. Every step is connected to the development of spiritual thinking.

♦ ♦ ♦

How would you like to be part of a church that was filled with people who were all taking these kinds of spiritual steps? Every one of these steps I've just mentioned is connected with a "divine moment." These are examples of a person taking a spiritual step of obedience, and there are more of them! In the Great Commission Jesus instructs us to teach people within the church "to **obey everything** I have commanded you" (Matt. 28:20, emphasis added). He says, "Whoever has my commands and obeys them, he is the one who loves me" (John 14:21).

The promise of Jesus is that for Christians who obey His commands, He and the Father will come to them and "make our home" with them (v. 23). What an incredible promise for me and for you. A healthy church understands these spiritual steps of obedience, the "divine moments" the church needs from God. People like me and you must learn to pray specifically and expect these moments to happen in our lives! Each of us learns to obey God quickly when He speaks to us. Our obedience will dramatically affect the people around us. Every spiritual step we take helps create a climate where God can talk to other people within our church. When we take these steps of obedience, we become mature, global Christians!

What kind of divine moments do you need in your personal life? What divine moments does your local church need from God? Have you identified them? Are you regularly and specifically praying for them to happen to you and those around you?

◆ ◆ ◆

**It is divine moments from God that
create a healthy church.**

◆ ◆ ◆

When Paul talks about our spiritual resources, he says they have incredible power to "demolish strongholds," and are needed *even in the lives of good people like you and me.* Within the church, he offers an additional insight when he writes: "take captive every thought to make it obedient to Christ" (2 Cor. 10:5). Here we see it again—God is highly interested in the way we think. God uses the church to help people take spiritual steps, and every step is connected to the development of spiritual thinking. This is the process the Holy Spirit uses to lead all of our thinking to become obedient to the thinking of Christ (1 Cor. 2:16; Phil. 2:5).

When a church has people who are taking these spiritual

steps of obedience and is developing people who think spiritually, church health happens naturally. We can help create the climate, but God alone does the work (John 15:5). The health of a local church is directly linked to the thinking and spiritual obedience of the individual Christians like you and me. When we correctly teach and when people do what our Lord commands them to do within His church (Matt. 28:20), a healthy church is the natural result.

Emphasizing Church Health over Church Growth

In the last 35 years there has been a lot of writing on the subject of church growth. Growing churches have been studied all over the world, to find out the characteristics and causes of their growth. Some of this focus has resulted in increased effectiveness and the spiritual growth of the church. But along with it has come significant criticism from people who feel that a study of "church growth" alone does not accurately reflect the spiritual emphasis the church needs.

◆ ◆ ◆

Other things replace our hunger to experience divine moments from God. The church does not stop believing in divine moments; they just stop happening because they are no longer our focus.

◆ ◆ ◆

As a result, as we enter the 21st century, there has been a shift in focus from church growth to church health. We believe Rick Warren is right when he states, "The key issue for churches in the twenty-first century will be church health, not church growth."[5] This is a much-needed biblical emphasis. Both Jesus and Paul seemed very interested, not only in the quantity of the crowd, but also in the quality of individual spiritual obedience.

In his best-selling book *Fresh Wind, Fresh Fire,* Jim Cymbala correctly warn us of the three things most people think about when asked how their church is doing. They usually respond with an answer that includes something like this: "Attendance is about 150, we've just finished remodeling our building, and our cash income this year is going to be about $175,000." Cymbala writes, "Attendance, buildings and cash. A-B-C: The new holy trinity."[6]

While all of these things are important considerations for a local church, the problem we face is when these things capture our heart and become the focal point. We do not mean for it to happen, but when our attendance, buildings, and cash become the focus, they begin replacing our hunger to experience divine moments from God. Usually churches do not stop believing in God's work through divine moments. Our church having divine moments just stops happening because they are no longer the primary focus that we have. We do not depend on them taking place, because we can operate our church and corporately survive without them. Over time in numbers of local churches and judicatories, our gatherings ultimately become no different from a secular business or social service agency. It is then appropriate to write Ichabod over the door of the church, for "the glory has departed" (1 Sam. 4:21).

Paul reminds all of us within the church that everything we build is one day going to be tested. "Each builder must choose with care how to build. . . . the work of each builder will become visible . . . it will be revealed with fire, and the fire will test what sort of work each has done" (1 Cor. 3:10, 13, NRSV). At New Church Specialties (NCS), we have discovered there is no relationship between the size of a church and the health of a church. We can take you to churches with 50 people in attendance where divine moments are happening and spiritual steps of obedience are taking place. We can take you to churches with 350 or 1,350 in attendance where no divine moments are happening. The reverse can also be true. Churches running 1,350 or 350 can be filled with spiritual steps of obedience and churches with 50 in attendance can be a place where spiritual thinking is absent. There is no relationship between size and health. We need all sizes of churches. Some people like large churches, and others like small ones. What we are committed to assist the development of are genuinely healthy churches, large and small, that cultivate spiritual thinking and maintain a focus on divine moments from God.

Maintaining Spiritual Dependence

I am a deep believer in a church developing action plans, strategies, and healthy structures. All of our human efforts are designed to create a healthy climate where God can do His work. Do we believe it is important to do our part? *Yes!* But we must never forget it is *God alone* who does the work of building a healthy church. *God alone* causes people to take spiritual steps of obedience, not us.

Paul understood this well when he wrote, "I planted the seed, Apollos watered it, but God made it grow. So neither he who plants nor he who waters is anything, but only God, who makes things grow" (1 Cor. 3:6-7). None of our human efforts can create a healthy church. To think otherwise is heresy. We do not create church health by the planning we teach church leaders to do at New Church University or any other human effort. "We are [simply] God's fellow workers" in His church (v. 9).

We must always make certain in our ministries that we keep Jesus in His rightful place. In everything we do, He is the One who must become greater, and "church health" must be seen in its proper place as being a means to an end, but not the end itself. John clearly understood himself as simply a tool in leading people to Christ. He said, "No one can receive anything except what has been given from heaven. . . . He must increase, but I must decrease" (John 3:27, 30, NRSV).

The end objective of everything we do is to cooperate with the Holy Spirit in creating a climate where God comes, changes a person's thinking, and leads him or her to take spiritual steps of obedience. These spiritual steps happen in divine moments. It is all the work of God! It is these divine moments that create a healthy church.

3
I · LOVE TO · BE CORRECTED BY · THE WORD · OF · GOD

"All Scripture is God-breathed and is useful for *teaching, rebuking,* correcting *and training in righteousness"* *(2 Tim. 3:16, emphasis added).*

DO YOU REMEMBER BEING CORRECTED when you were a child? Did you love it? You probably did not. Left to ourselves, none of us loves to be corrected (Prov. 29:19). The Bible has a lot to say about correction. It teaches in Proverbs that if we ignore correction, we will lead others astray (10:17), if we hate correction we are stupid (12:1), if we heed correction we will be honored (13:18), and we show prudence and good sense (15:5). Mockers resent correction and will not consult those who are wise (v. 12). "Whoever heeds correction gains understanding" (v. 32).

◆ ◆ ◆

In your spiritual life in God's church, do you regularly seek to be corrected by God?

◆ ◆ ◆

Jeremiah went through some great difficulties in following God's will for his life. He certainly had the right attitude when he wrote, "I know, O LORD, that the way of human beings is not in their control, that mortals as they walk cannot direct their steps. *Correct me, O LORD*" (Jer. 10:23-24, NRSV, emphasis added). Let me ask you, in your spiritual life in God's church, do you regularly seek to be corrected by God?

◆ ◆ ◆

There is a direct relationship between spiritual maturity and the attitude of being teachable.

◆ ◆ ◆

There is a direct relationship between spiritual maturity and the attitude of being teachable. People who spiritually grow want to learn. They seek wisdom and desire to be corrected by God in any way that makes them wiser. Proverbs instructs us: "If you had responded to my rebuke, I [wisdom] would have poured out my heart to you and made my thoughts known to you" (1:23); "if you correct those who care about life . . . they'll love you for it!" (9:8, TM); "Give instruction to the wise, and they will become wiser still; teach the righteous and they will gain in learning" (9:9, NRSV); "the wise in heart accept commands" (10:8); "Fools are headstrong and do what they like; wise people take advice" (12:15, TM); "Pride only breeds quarrels, but wisdom is found in those who take advice" (13:10).

Jesus Teaches on Biblical Correction

Remember what Jesus teaches? He always keeps calling us to take personal steps of obedience (John 14:21), to go and make disciples of all nations (Matt. 28:19), to follow His example of seeking the lost (Luke 15:1-10), to continually trust in the power of the Holy Spirit, and to be regularly corrected by His Word (Matt. 22:29).

Jesus was a master communicator, a master at using one-liners. He could take a complex issue and, in a short statement, give a solution people would never forget. Here is one example. The Pharisees were laying plans to trap Jesus in what He said. They came to Him, filled with duplicity. "Teacher, we know that you are sincere, and teach the way of God in accordance with truth, and show deference to no one; for you do not regard people with partiality" (Matt. 22:16, NRSV). It was obvious these people hated Jesus and wanted Him out of the way.

◆ ◆ ◆

Jesus was a master communicator. He could take a complex issue and in a short statement, give a solution people would never forget.

◆ ◆ ◆

Here came the trick question, "Tell us then, what is your opinion? Is it right to pay taxes to Caesar or not?" (Matt. 22:17). From a human standpoint, Jesus was in a no-win situation. Roman soldiers were standing on one side of the crowd. If Jesus told the people it was not right to pay taxes, the soldiers would be up in arms because their salaries were paid by those taxes. If Jesus said they should pay taxes, the people would be up in arms because they hated paying taxes to Rome.

◆ ◆ ◆

Jesus taught, "You are in error because you do not know the Scriptures or the power of God."

◆ ◆ ◆

How did Jesus communicate in this no-win situation? He did it with a one-line statement. He replied (in modern language), "Does anyone have a quarter?" He held it up to the crowd, pointing to the face on the front, "Whose picture is this?" When they replied, "Caesar's," Jesus gave a one-liner most Christians in North America have memorized: "Give to Caesar what is Caesar's, and to God what is God's" (Matt. 22:21). As a master communicator, Jesus understood the power of God-inspired thoughts, stories, and short statements.

◆ ◆ ◆

Individuals and the church as a whole regularly need repentance and correction.

◆ ◆ ◆

You would think after watching what had just transpired, the Sadducees would realize Jesus was more than a match for them. But here they came trying to baffle Jesus with a story about a man who was married to a woman, and later died. His brother married the woman, and he also died. After three funerals, all I can say is that the fourth brother was crazy! After the sixth brother died, can you imagine the emotions of the seventh brother walking up the aisle?

As the story goes, all seven married the woman and all seven brothers died. The question the Sadducees asked Jesus was: "In the resurrection, who gets the woman?" When Jesus heard this story (as a master communicator), He responded with a one-liner that should be etched in the memory of every Christian and never forgotten. It is the solution related to almost every issue involving spiritual maturity and helping our church become healthy. "Jesus answered, 'You're off base on two counts: You don't know your Bibles, and you don't know how God works'" (Matt. 22:29, TM).

I want to suggest that nearly every time our church has a

problem, an error, or the need for correction in some way, either we do not understand the Scriptures or we are not trusting the power of the Holy Spirit. The church regularly needs repentance and correction. This is what Jesus taught.

Maintaining an Openness to Change

♦ ♦ ♦

A prerequisite to ReFocusing is repentance, brokenness, and developing a sense of urgency to be different.

♦ ♦ ♦

Paul writes, "All Scripture is God-breathed and is useful for teaching, rebuking, *correcting* and training in righteousness" (2 Tim. 3:16, emphasis added). As I attend church, one of the main purposes of the Bible is to regularly correct me. If I am a maturing Christian taking spiritual steps of obedience, it may not be easy. But every Sunday when I gather to worship, my attitude will be, "Lord, I want to be corrected today by the Word of God. Would You teach me, guide me, reveal to me the changes You want me to make in my life today?"

As we work with churches in ReFocusing, we are finding a prerequisite to ReFocusing is repentance, brokenness, and developing a sense of urgency to be different. "A broken spirit; a broken and contrite heart, O God, you will not despise" (Ps. 51:17). Every maturing Christian taking spiritual steps of obedience will seek to be corrected as often as he or she can, by the Word of God.

♦ ♦ ♦

If I am a maturing Christian, I will have regular changes of mind and corresponding changes in my life.

♦ ♦ ♦

The Greek word for repent is *metanoia*, which means "a change of mind and a corresponding change of life." It is not just horrible sinners outside God's church who need to repent and be corrected by God. If I am a maturing Christian taking spiritual steps of obedience, the Holy Spirit will regularly prompt my thinking to change. I will have regular changes of mind and corresponding changes in my life. I will never stop growing and maturing. I will never feel that I have spiritually arrived. God will continue showing me how I can take more steps toward becoming a global Christian who sees the world every day through the eyes of Jesus. I then will remain humble, broken, and teachable before God. How many people like this would you like to have in your church?

4

WHAT · THE CHURCH · IS ... AND CAN · BE

"His intent was that now, through the church, *the manifold wisdom of God should be made known"*
(Eph. 3:10, emphasis added).

♦ ♦ ♦

Partial truth ultimately leads to incorrect beliefs and spiritually immature behavior.

♦ ♦ ♦

WE NEED TO APPROACH THE SUBJECT of what the church is and can be with a deep sense of awe and reverence. This is holy ground. We want God to correct our thinking about the church if in any way our thinking is not in line with His Word. We must begin by examining the religious thought of much of the North American church as compared to the practical doctrine of the church taught in the New Testament. Western culture has emphasized the freedom of the individual and his or her personal relationship with God. If this emphasis on the individual is not balanced with a correct teaching about Christian community, Christians will live with only partial truth. Partial truth ultimately leads to wrong thinking, incorrect beliefs, and spiritually immature behavior. Sad to say, this spiritual problem is found all over North America, both inside and outside local congregations.

What Is the Church?

♦ ♦ ♦

We must teach our generation it is God's will
that they embrace, fall in love with,
and give themselves up for the imperfect group of
people Christ gave himself up for—the church!

♦ ♦ ♦

What is the church? Let me offer a practical definition. The visible church is an imperfect group of Christ-followers who have been gathered by the Holy Spirit who assemble regularly for worship and the administration of the sacraments[7] and who seek correction from God's Word. These Christian followers proclaim the gospel by locking arms with each other and providing a witness to their community and the world that they are one with Jesus and the Father (John 17:21-23). They cooperate with the wider church to fulfill Christ's global mission of making disciples of all nations.

I would never presume to suggest that in this brief paragraph we can summarize or clarify the volumes that have been written in the last 2,000 years about the church. But literally millions of North American Christians need solid teaching and correction on this issue. What we believe about the church is foundational to our spiritual future.

Jesus Loves Imperfect Churches

As lay and clergy church leaders, we have all heard people make comments about the imperfections of the church. Many of the reasons people give for not participating in God's church flow out of a spirit of criticism. There are millions of people today who say they love Jesus; their problem is with the imperfect people who regularly attend church.

Our call as church leaders is to teach our generation it is God's will that they embrace, fall in love with, and give themselves up for the imperfect group of people Christ gave himself up for—the church. Although Jesus and God are both perfect, the church, the physical expression of Jesus in the world today, is not perfect. We must teach this is *not* a surprise or a discouragement to God. He is always doing more underneath than we can see on the surface.

Jesus knew His church would be imperfect when He planted and regularly refocused the very first one in Jerusalem. If you feel like you have problems with your church, look at the problems Jesus dealt with.

1. The treasurer was stealing money from Him (John 12:6).
2. One of His key church leaders betrayed Him (Luke 22:47-48).
3. When He needed His leadership team, they slept (Matt. 26:40).
4. When pressured, the leadership team deserted Him (Matt. 26:55-56).
5. His closest key leader disowned Him (Matt. 26:75).

◆ ◆ ◆

When I fall in love with the church, I am falling in love with the institution God has chosen to bring salvation to the world and the vehicle He is using to prepare me to meet Him.

◆ ◆ ◆

Several encouraging truths stand out as we evaluate the problems in the church with which Jesus worked. If your church treasurer is not stealing from your church, if you are not being betrayed by other church people, if only half of your church sleeps during meetings, if all the people in your church are not deserting you, and if your closest friend has not disowned you, you are doing better than Jesus did!

If you have seen the movie *The Passion of the Christ,* replay the scenes in your mind again. The treasurer is stealing money; a friend is betraying Jesus; when He needs people the most, they cannot stay awake; when His key friends do wake up, they desert Him; and His closest friend denies knowing Him with a string of curses. Here is the question. Would you go to the Cross for that group of people? Would you give yourself up in sacrifice for that kind of imperfect church? Jesus did.

If these things happened to Jesus in the church He led, we can certainly expect there will be many kinds of problems every other Christian will have who follows Jesus. Jesus had a group of very imperfect people. Even though they hurt Him, Jesus gave himself up for them. He gave himself up for the church (Eph. 5:25). He did this because He knew *the only way* local churches would become healthy all over the world is for people to follow His example and give themselves up for their church.

A God-Chosen Institution

♦ ♦ ♦

There is no plan B. We are it. God has chosen to use us to bring His salvation to the planet!

♦ ♦ ♦

We have been taught in North America that salvation is an individual choice we make, but God's Word teaches that Jesus sacrificed himself for *more* than just my individual sin. Jesus died for the church, for He realized that only when I as a Christian walk in harmony with God's church, can I be made "holy and blameless" by God's Word as I should (Eph. 5:27). When I fall in love with the church, I am falling in love with the institution God has chosen to bring salvation to the world, and the vehicle He is using to prepare me to meet Him.

The church has and always will live in tension. She celebrates what God has done so far, but she also longs to be perfect like Christ. In this world, she is not perfect. She is moving toward being "without stain or wrinkle or any other blemish" (v. 27). This is the vision of Jesus for your church. As your church is regularly washed with God's Word and the people within your church take spiritual steps of obedience, the church is able to move from the wrinkled stage to the radiant stage!

The Bible says, "His intent was that now, *through the church,* the manifold wisdom of God should be made known" (3:10, emphasis added). God's intent is to make His wisdom and revelation known through your church and hundreds of thousands of other churches like it. There is no plan B. We are it. He has chosen to use us to bring His salvation to the planet.

The people the Holy Spirit has gathered in your church are not perfect, and they never will be totally perfect until they get to heaven. Jesus has a lot more "correcting" to do on them just as He does on you and me. Jesus loves your church and has a clear plan to make her holy as He cleanses her week by week with correct teaching from His Word (5:25-26).

Jesus in the Flesh

Paul says, "In the same way a husband and wife are 'one flesh,' I want to give you a profound mystery—Jesus and His church have become one flesh as well." Jesus is so committed to your church that He has united and become "one flesh" with her (see v. 32).

What does this mean in a practical sense? When you see Mary Lou (a widow) sitting on the third row, left side this Sunday morning, you are seeing Jesus in the flesh. When you see Mark and Becky sitting on the fifth row, right side this Sunday morning, you are seeing Jesus in the flesh. It is the Holy Spirit himself who has drawn Mary Lou, Mark, and Becky together within your church. Every week you gather, Jesus is among you! It is so important that you understand why He prayed for you the way He did before He went to the Cross (John 17:20-23). What your church is part of is so much larger and more incredible than what you visibly see every week. It is bigger than all of us. It is eternal!

◆ ◆ ◆

What your church is part of is so much larger and more incredible than what you visibly see every week. It is bigger than all of us. It is eternal!

◆ ◆ ◆

How can you and I think more correctly about the church as we come to worship each week? You and I know many people who have been around the church all their lives, yet some of them may not act as spiritually mature as others who have been around the church just a few months. There is a big difference between *growing old* in the Lord and *growing up* in the Lord. Nowhere is this more apparent than in the way some Christians act in relationship to the visible church.

Fourteen Truths About the Visible Church

We choose to use the term *visible church* because many people in our culture want to identify with Jesus and the *invisible* church. They believe they can be good Christians and never attend church. They church-hop and church-shop but never stop. These professing Christians do great damage to Christ's church, especially as their actions become socially acceptable to larger numbers of people. Both Gallup and Barna research polls reveal there are tens of millions of Americans who claim a personal faith in Christ but have no commitment to any visible church.

◆ ◆ ◆

In Early Church teaching, it is inconceivable that someone could be a Christian and not be a vital part of a visible, local body of Christ.

◆ ◆ ◆

In the Bible, the word *church* is used two ways. First, it is used to refer to every Christian that has ever lived in time. This is the church universal, and the word *church* is used this way in the Bible four times. The other 110 times it is used in the Bible, the word *church* refers to a visible, local body of believers. The church at Corinth, the church at Philippi, the church at Thessalonica—these were all visible, local bodies in which individual Christians were expected to become a vital part.

In Early Church teaching, it is inconceivable that someone could be a Christian and not be a vital part of a visible, local body of Christ. Dozens of commands given to Christians in the New Testament cannot be obeyed unless we are an active part of a visible church. Every week I attend worship, I need to regularly remind myself of the nature and purpose of the church. What follows is a list of 14 things the Bible teaches us about the visible church.

◆ ◆ ◆

God is the one who created the church. To say that I am a Christian and not regularly assemble with God's people is to deny what God has created and called me to be.

◆ ◆ ◆

1. **The visible church is a divine community.** God is the one who created the church. It is not a "Christian option." Every Christian should join and actively participate in a visible church. To say that I am a Christian and not regularly assemble with God's people is to deny what God has created and called me to be (Heb. 10:25; Eph. 1:4-23; 2:12-22; 1 Pet. 2:9).

2. **The visible church is where Christ is present and at work.** "Where two or three are gathered in my name, there am I with them" (Matt. 18:20). Healthy churches have a profound awareness of the Lord's presence as they gather each week. Large churches or small, when we come together in the name of Christ, Jesus is at work. Divine moments happen and spiritual steps of obedience are taken.

3. **The visible church and Jesus were one at Pentecost.** Through the outpouring of the Holy Spirit and spiritual presence of Jesus, the preaching and teaching of Jesus greatly multiplied through His followers. They were truly one (John 17:21), and the world came to believe. From the beginning, the church and Jesus were never separated in any Christian's thinking. The great Early Church father Ignatius wrote, "Where Christ is, there is the church."[8]

◆ ◆ ◆

If you are a Christian, you are to become a vital part of Christ's visible body and make it better. No cop-outs allowed!

◆ ◆ ◆

4. **The visible church and Jesus are still one today!** The actions of the church are and should be the actions of Christ. What Jesus began while He was in the flesh, the church now has taken on the responsibility to fulfill. He is the Head of the church. We are His body in the world, His hands, His feet, His voice, His heart. No one is perfect, but if you are a Chris-

tian, you are to become a vital part of His visible body and make it better (1 Cor. 12:27). No cop-outs allowed!

5. **The visible church is what Jesus died for.** Jesus did not just die for individuals; He died for your church. He "gave himself up" (Eph. 5:25) so your church could be holy (Heb. 12:12).

6. **The visible church is what Jesus will return for.** Jesus will return for the believers from your church, and they will be joined together with Him for all eternity (Rev. 19:7-9; 1 Thess. 4:13-18).

◆ ◆ ◆

The church is where I am regularly washed with the water of God's Word and challenged to become more like Him.

◆ ◆ ◆

7. **The visible church will never be perfect in this life.** The church Jesus founded was full of imperfection. Paul wrote, "But when perfection comes, the imperfect disappears. . . . Now we see but a poor reflection as in a mirror" (1 Cor. 13:10, 12). It is the calling of Christian leaders to offer correct teaching so the church can move from wrinkled to radiant (Eph. 5:27).

◆ ◆ ◆

If I do not use my God-given gifts to help build up Christ's church, the church and the work of Jesus in the world will not be what it could be. Every little part matters a lot.

◆ ◆ ◆

8. **The visible church is where I spiritually mature in Christlikeness.** The church is the institution God has chosen to help prepare me for service to the world and the vehicle He

is using to prepare me to meet Him. It is where I am regularly washed with the water of His Word and challenged to become more like Him.

9. **The visible church is my spiritual family.** Paul writes, "Let us do good to all people, especially to those who belong to the family of believers" (Gal. 6:10). Did you know that your spiritual family, the church, will last longer than your physical family? You will be in the family of the church forever.

10. **The visible church is where I discover and use my spiritual gifts.** "Now about spiritual gifts, brothers, I do not want you to be ignorant" (1 Cor. 12:1). "Each one should use whatever gift he has received to serve others" (1 Pet. 4:10). If I do not use my God-given spiritual gifts to help build up Christ's church, the church and Jesus' work in the world will not be what it could be. Every little part matters a lot (Eph. 4:16).

11. **The visible church is where I receive spiritual protection.** The Bible commands pastors, "Keep watch over . . . the flock, of which the Holy Spirit has made you overseers. Be shepherds of the church of God. . . . savage wolves will come in among you . . . and distort the truth" (Acts 20:28-30). Part of the church and pastors' responsibility is to help the flock separate truth from error.

♦ ♦ ♦

The visible church helps me fulfill Christ's Great Commission by linking arms with the wider church, enabling me to become a global Christian.

♦ ♦ ♦

12. **The visible church provides me with spiritual accountability.** The Bible says, "Brothers, if someone is caught in a sin, you who are spiritual should restore him gently. . . . Carry each other's burdens, and in this way you will fulfill the law of Christ" (Gal. 6:1-2). The reason numbers of people do

not join a church is because they do not want to be held accountable for personal growth and change. This is a spiritual maturity and obedience issue.

13. **The visible church helps me fulfill Christ's Great Commission.** Every Christian is called to "make disciples of all nations" (Matt. 28:19). Separate and isolated, I cannot be the global Christian I should be. It is by linking arms with the wider church, sending and supporting her missionaries, that I am privileged to actively participate in the church as a global movement.

14. **The visible church has many "tribes" God is using today.** Many different denominations adhere to the basic tenets of the Christian faith and are faithful to witness Jesus Christ as their Lord. Christians do not have to "see eye to eye" on every issue to be able to "walk hand in hand."

This is what the church is . . . and can be! The Head of the church is calling you to become a vital part of His visible army. Do not be like the soldier who says, "I want to fight in the war. I just do not want to be a part of any specific platoon. I will fight wherever I want to, on my own." The Bible instructs us, "No one serving as a soldier gets involved in civilian affairs—he wants to please his commanding officer" (2 Tim. 2:4).

◆ ◆ ◆

Will you sign up and show up for active duty in your local church? Eternal issues hang in the balance. Now is the time for you to say yes.

◆ ◆ ◆

The Bible teaches that the church cannot operate with you remaining uninvolved in Christ's visible church; He expects you to enlist. The stakes are high. The battle lines are drawn. The community you live in, the extended area you are part of, and the world waits for your response. Will you sign up and show up for active duty in your local church? Eternal issues hang in the balance. Now is the time for you to say yes.

5
A · Case
· for
Connection

"Obey your leaders and submit to them, for they are keeping watch over your souls and will give an account. Let them do this with joy and not with sighing—for that would be harmful to you" (Heb. 13:17, NRSV).

If you are part of a denominational family, the probability is high that at some time in your life you have thought about "becoming independent." If you are part of a judicatory that has any kind of history or tradition, you have probably been tempted to separate yourself from it. I have spoken to dozens of strong, entrepreneurial Christians in the past several years, and when I relay my experience on this subject, every one of them knows the feeling and can identify with the issues we are addressing here. Christians with great potential are usually those who live on the edge, not those who "play it safe." Leaders with great potential usually reject the status quo and question "why we do what we do, the way we do it." If church leaders are prudent, they will learn how to wisely manage entrepreneurially oriented laypersons and leverage their abilities for the health of the church.

Understanding Spiritual Legacy

◆ ◆ ◆

Even if a church closes its doors in the future,
its spiritual legacy never dies!

◆ ◆ ◆

It seems to me the best way to teach the subject of commitment to a denominational family is to simply share the lessons God has taught me on my own journey. I would encourage you sometime to do a study on the theme of spiritual heritage. We all have one. It may stretch down through several generations, or if you are a first-generation Christian, your personal heritage within the church may be just beginning. David talks about this spiritual legacy we are given by those before us and writes, "God; you have given me the heritage of those who fear your name" (Ps. 61:5).

Spiritual legacy is built over time. It includes a large number of very typical Sundays. Many Sunday mornings seem to be no different from the previous week for the faithful who show up. When they arrive, worship, and serve, they have no idea how their faithfulness will create a spiritual legacy. They do not know how their ordinary spiritual routine will touch a family, a generation, even future generations of Christians yet to be born.

They come together as a group of imperfect people who believe in Jesus. They gather regularly with each other in this God-created group called the church. They meet every week for prayer, teaching, encouragement, and correction from God's Word. They lock arms with each other to provide a witness to their community and the world. Through their faithfulness to Christ across the years, they pour spiritual legacy into the life of every person who attends. The people who are touched carry the legacy with them to their graves. Even if the local church where they meet should ever close it doors in the future, the legacy never dies! This spiritual heritage the church offers to people has an eternal impact.

Dr. Bill Sullivan reminds us that every church currently in existence in North America started out as church plant, offering a spiritual legacy. "Anytime anywhere people worship or serve in a church . . . they benefit from the efforts of some church starter and core group who began their church. Every church . . . stands as a memorial to someone's vision, sacrifice and sweat. Some sold farms. Some quit jobs. Some went out under the sky to preach with no security. . . . Someone paid a great price to begin your church. Never forget it. And everyone who has come to faith as a result of that church must feel a debt of gratitude to those selfless folks who started it. They were persons of amazing vision, tenacity and faith."[9]

♦ ♦ ♦

They unlocked the doors, turned on the lights, rang the bell, and prayed for the people. They had no idea how their faithfulness would create a spiritual legacy.

♦ ♦ ♦

How My Spiritual Legacy Began

I had the fortunate privilege of a great spiritual heritage given to me through a small country church in Kurtz, Indiana. The town of Kurtz has a population of only 125 people. The church began very small and has never really been large. There are literally tens of thousands of churches, connected with multiple denominations all over North America that are just like the Kurtz church.

The Kurtz church was organized as a denominationally connected church back in 1920. The church began out of a series of religious meetings just like thousands of other churches in America. A group of committed Christians traveled to Kurtz from Seymour, Indiana. They put up a tent and preached in the "Kurtz Grove" for several weeks as an outreach to people who were non-Christians or not active in a church. They held a membership class after the meeting was over, and according to church records, 12 people joined. If you believe the Bible's teaching, it was the Holy Spirit who drew those people together to form that small country church.

Back in her beginning, the Kurtz church did not have what she has today. There was no limestone parsonage, fine fellowship hall, padded pews, or indoor plumbing. But what that small group of believers had when they came together was a sense of God's presence, the working of the Holy Spirit, and a mission to lock arms and touch those outside the church with Christ's love. The faithful people in this country church showed up every Sunday morning for worship. They unlocked the doors, turned on the lights, rang the bell, and prayed for unchurched people by name. For 16 years they did that, and the church grew from 12 to 60 people in attendance.

◆ ◆ ◆

With every life transformation, spiritual legacy is formed and spiritual heritage is established. It took me a number of years and some spiritual maturing to understand this.

◆ ◆ ◆

It was a Sunday morning in the spring of 1936. Two young girls, ages two and one, were playing outside on their farm near Kurtz. Their father, a young farmer named David Whitredge, was plowing behind a team of horses out in his field that morning. It had been his custom to work on Sunday rather than attending church. He had not been raised in a Christian home. His father was an alcoholic, his parents were divorced when he was 12, and he had moved to southern Indiana to live with his uncle. He met and married a schoolteacher who was also unchurched. Together they bought a farm outside of Kurtz. Spiritual influence in their lives did not exist until some people from this young church in Kurtz started to call on them. They invited David and his wife to worship. They urged him to consider raising his two girls in the church. They started praying for him regularly by name.

Plowing out in the field that morning David heard the church bell ring. He had heard it on Sundays before. But the people of the church had been praying. A divine moment happened. He suddenly had a change of mind, a change in his thinking! In answer to their prayers, he stopped plowing, took the team of horses back to the barn, went to the house, and said to his wife, Fern, "Get the girls ready. Today, we are going to visit that church." The morning he walked in, the Holy Spirit was present. Another divine moment happened. David Whitredge, along with his wife, Fern, committed his life to Christ that morning.

You may be wondering why that morning in 1936 is so meaningful in my life. The one-year-old girl David and Fern took to church that day ultimately became my mother. Ps. 103:17 says, "But from everlasting to everlasting the LORD's love is with those who fear him, and his righteousness with their children's children." God used the church to touch my grandfather's life, and his decision that day transformed future generations in our family.

In 1946, my dad's family began attending the Kurtz church. That is how he met my mother. In 1953, Fern was sustained by the church when David was killed in a tractor accident while plowing on the farm. I was born in 1956 into that country church. I have heard many stories from my relatives about my grandfather. Although I never met him physically, I have heard much about him spiritually. I am told he was a real leader of men, a man's man and a strong Christian lay leader. One thing I am told repeatedly is that he loved the church. After his conversion to Christ, he was zealous in encouraging others all over the county to attend. He became Sunday School superintendent, and at one point the Kurtz church had an attendance of over 250 people. For 17 years he created a spiritual legacy that he passed on to me, though we never met.

If we had the time to research it and the venue to share it, every Christian reading this book could tell a similar story about the way God has used the imperfect, visible church to touch and transform your family. With every transformation, with every divine moment, spiritual legacy is formed. A spiritual heritage is established. It took me a number of years and some spiritual maturing to fully understand and appreciate this.

Managing Entrepreneurial People

♦ ♦ ♦

Because I did not understand agenda harmony,
a highly influential lay leader caused a church split
and a group of people walked out the door
with 40 percent of the church's income.

♦ ♦ ♦

When you have Christians out on the edge in ministry, reaching new people for Jesus, experimenting with new approaches, testing the status quo, people who live by the letter of the denominational structure usually feel uncomfortable. At this point, we have a choice to make. When we create a flexible climate that not only allows but encourages entrepreneurial creativity in ministry, we thrive. If we choose to restrict and create a strong climate of control, we choose to die.

I am grateful God placed me in a denominational family that encourages entrepreneurial activity most of the time.

I have a personal experience pertaining to this. The year was 1989. I was serving in our third church plant and greatly "stretching the envelope" for the judicatory of which I was a member. My wife and I had started the church with only two people besides our family. The Lord blessed, however, and the church was growing rapidly in an upper-middle-income community. We were 15 months into the project. We were worshiping in a school and had moved the church office out of our home into a multiroom office in a nearby business park. We had hired a full-time worship and administration pastor, a part-time office manager, and from the first day had continued to give 10 percent of our income away to missions through our denominational family.

Our judicatory had given us a total of $13,800 to begin the church. The fact that we financially survived was a miracle in itself. The level of energy and sacrifice to start a new church from the ground up with few resources is enormous. At the same time, many people within the judicatory viewed what we were doing with high degrees of suspicion. Our church was very different in style from a number of the other churches in the judicatory family.

♦ ♦ ♦

God never wastes a hurt if we are willing to learn from it.

♦ ♦ ♦

Several pastors wrote letters to the judicatory leader complaining about our ministry, and copies were sent to me to read. I wish I could tell you that I responded to these criticisms with a high degree of spiritual maturity. I am sorry to say, I did not. Looking back on it, I was a very difficult church planter to manage. Some of the decisions I made and the things I said to those in spiritual leadership over me were not filled with either wisdom or tact. Much of the conflict was the result of my own immaturity.

How God Taught Me to Love the Church

Even though I never spoke openly with our leadership team about the conflict, the people closest to me could sense my frustration. I will never forget the night that "the discussion" occurred. One of the men in the church was a builder who had helped my wife and I build a small new home, the very first one we had ever owned. We had just moved in, and about 10 people from the leadership team were meeting in our living room. With the exception of one, all of them had no previous background with the denomination that had sponsored us.

◆ ◆ ◆

For the first time, I saw the gap between the attitude Jesus had toward the church and the attitude I had. The gap was massive!

◆ ◆ ◆

Sensing my frustration, a discussion ensued about our denominational connection. This was before the church was formally chartered and organized, so the only ties we had with the church were the ties I had personally. One of them finally asked, "Larry, why do you stay with your denomination? Is it the retirement program?" Another offered, "If you would like to consider going independent, we could gather the resources beginning tonight that would secure your retirement."

Because I did not fully understand agenda harmony, when we came down to organize as a denominationally connected church, a highly influential lay leader who did not want the connection caused a church split, and a group of people walked out the door with 40 percent the church's income. The attack by this group on my personal character was one of the most difficult things I have ever experienced. It caused a great deal of emotional pain for my wife, Denise, and our family.

◆ ◆ ◆

When I really saw it for the first time, I knew it was worth it to give the rest of my life for the church.

◆ ◆ ◆

I have learned so much about the church over the last 25 years. God never wastes a hurt if we are willing to learn from it. People have asked me where I developed my understanding of the church and what motivated me to study what the Bible says about the church. They ask how I came to put our teaching on "Falling in Love with the Church" at the center of New Church University training. My response is always the same. When I came within a hair's breadth of leaving my denominational family, when I was in pain and felt all alone, at that point I was forced to study what it was I was willing to give my life up for. In my own pain I read passages like, "Fix [your] eyes on Jesus . . . you have not yet resisted to the point of shedding your blood" (Heb. 12:2, 4). I read what Jesus went through with the church leadership team with whom He worked. I read how He was rejected and cursed and still "gave himself up for" the church (Eph. 5:25).

◆ ◆ ◆

I have watched enough people in ministry over the years to learn that impulsive decisions to separate when we are younger are usually regretted when we are older.

◆ ◆ ◆

As I read, I began looking at my own heart. I began to see my own critical spirit, my rigid perspective, and my judgmental attitudes. It took a lot for God to get my attention so that spiritual maturity could start happening inside my soul. For the first time in my life, I saw a gap between the attitude Jesus had toward the church and the attitude I had. The gap was so massive! I was so far from what the Bible taught a right attitude toward God's church should be. That is where my real repentance and brokenness before God began. When I gave Him permission, Jesus began putting His finger on every attitude I held that He wanted to change in my relationship to the church.

When I began to look at the church through His eyes rather than just my own, my heart began a gigantic adjustment. What do you think Jesus saw when He was on the Cross? What was He thinking when He hung there suspended between two worlds in agony with His life's blood oozing out of His veins? We only know a few words Jesus spoke before He died. But the Bible makes clear when Jesus died on the Cross, He "gave himself up," not just for individuals but for the church.

He had a vision of imperfect people like you and me all over the world, gathered into divine groups. Meeting every week. Being corrected and obedient to His Word. Locking arms with each other in ministry and witness to the world. What a divine strategy! What an incredible design! What a marvelous creation of God! When I really saw it for the first time, I knew it was worth it to give the rest of my life for the church.

Eleven Biblical and Practical Reasons for Connection

As I have studied both the Scriptures and church history, I have come to some conclusions about the imperfect visible church, denominational families, and the way God is working through all of these various "tribes." Because so much is at stake in our collective mission, I am a staunch advocate for congregations maintaining strong denominational connections. Let me offer 11 biblical and practical reasons why I have come to this conclusion.

1. **The Bible teaches Christians to be** *interdependent,* **not independent.** Paul describes the church as "the whole body, joined and held together by every supporting ligament, grow[ing] and build[ing] itself up in love" (Eph. 4:16). We never see in the scripture a case for separation. The climate for healthy witness to the world is always the prayer of Jesus, "that all of them may be one, Father" (John 17:21). In his impulsiveness, Paul had such a sharp disagreement with Barnabas that he parted company with him (Acts 15:39). In later and more mature years, Paul admitted it was his mistake (2 Tim. 4:11). I have watched enough people in ministry over the years to learn that impulsive decisions to separate ourselves when we are younger are usually regretted when we are older. We will talk about the few historical exceptions to this later.

◆ ◆ ◆

In the Old Testament, there were no independent Jews; everyone had a tribe.

◆ ◆ ◆

The concept above is widely accepted and understood in the secular world. Jesus taught that "the people of this world are more shrewd in dealing with their own kind than are the people of the light" (Luke 16:8). Business leaders flock to Steven Covey seminars and pay thousands of dollars to listen to him teach "interdependence is a higher value than independence."[10] This principle has its foundation in Scripture, and it should be lived out within the church.

2. **Many nondenominational fellowships act like denominational families.** During these past five years NCS has worked with 18 different denominational groups. We have also worked with church leaders from several nondenominational fellowships. It is our experience that nondenominational groups publish materials, have conferences together, find ways to help churches during pastoral transition, offer help when a local church is in crisis or has a moral failure, hold training events and conferences for ministers and lay leaders, provide schools for their young people, and find ways to send and support missionaries. These nondenominational fellowships certainly operate with a different form of church government compared to denominationally connected churches, but in many ways they act just like denominational families! They do so because they have learned across the years that achieving the mission of Christ requires Christians to lock arms and work together.

♦ ♦ ♦

Most separations today are not over burning spiritual issues but over polity, personality conflicts, or spiritual immaturity.

♦ ♦ ♦

3. **In the Old Testament, there were no independent Jews; everyone had a tribe.** The Bible teaches that the church is the new Israel of God (Gal. 6:16) and the fulfillment of the covenant God made with Abraham (Gen. 12:2-3; Gal. 3:8, 14-16). In many ways, denominational families can be likened to the Old Testament "tribes" of Israel. As you study the journey of God's people, God had everyone connected, there were no independent Jews! At times they did not get along with each other, and they certainly had their share of challenges, but they were all Israelites. They were all identified as the people

of God, and every one of them was connected to a tribal family.

4. **Denominations are in many ways like large spiritual families.** If you have ever been in a denominational family, have you noticed how many people know other people from across the country? People seem to all be related to each other. The wider body of Christ through a denomination offers Christians "family relationships" with other believers that extend far beyond the local church.

5. **In a few instances in church history, people have felt compelled to make decisions that caused them to separate from the visible church.** The Protestant Reformers like Martin Luther (Lutherans) and John Knox (Presbyterians) are examples. John Wesley, the father of Methodism, was a loyal member of the Church of England until his death. The Evangelical Awakening God created through John Wesley's life led to the founding of the Methodist church as a denomination after he died. As I have observed, however, there is a huge difference between these men and someone who leaves a denomination today. Most separations today are not over burning spiritual issues but over polity, personality conflicts, or spiritual immaturity.

God gives us a clear word that is not very popular these days in the North American church: "Obey your leaders and submit to them, for they are keeping watch over your souls and will give an account. Let them do this with joy and not with sighing—for that would be harmful to you" (Heb. 13:17, NRSV). Jesus teaches that there is a direct relationship between submission to authority and great faith (Matt. 8:5-10).

◆ ◆ ◆

Make your attitude toward the church positively contagious! God's promise is that you will find this to be of great personal advantage.

◆ ◆ ◆

I challenge you to be loyal to your judicatory and denominational family. It is the right thing to do. Submit to those God has placed in authority over you. Do your best to make their work "a real joy" because of their contact with you. Make your attitude about the church positively contagious! If you do, God's promise is that you will find this to be of great personal advantage (Heb. 13:17).

6. **The genius of connectedness to a denomination is that it provides local churches the opportunity to do together what no church can do separately.** Thousands of Southern Baptist Convention (SBC) churches have been started, missionaries have been sent, and Christian leaders have been educated and trained because of the Cooperative Program. The church polity of the SBC is built on a foundation of local church autonomy, and every church is congregational and independent, creating its own set of unique governmental challenges. Although there are some great Baptist churches God has raised up, the SBC Directors of Mission who have attended NCU all affirm there is no greatness as a spiritual movement without agenda harmony. Local churches must cooperate with other local churches for the Kingdom to multiply with great effectiveness.

The genius behind the thousands of Methodist churches that have multiplied is the cooperation of Methodism in apportionments and active connection to districts and conferences. Methodist churches working together do what no local church could ever do alone. My friend, Dr. Barry Carpenter, director of New Church and Congregational Development for the 900 churches in the Kentucky Conference, affirms that the secret of the Methodist movement historically has been its ability to gain agenda harmony for the health and multiplication of the church.

◆ ◆ ◆

People from different denominational families can
walk hand in hand without seeing eye to eye.

◆ ◆ ◆

NCS has its direct roots in both the Nazarene and Wesleyan denominations. Dr. Tom Nees oversees evangelism and church growth for the Church of the Nazarene, Dr. Jerry Pence oversees resourcing for The Wesleyan Church in a similar way—together they service 6,700 congregations in the U.S. and Canada. Both Dr. Nees and Dr. Pence affirm the principle that the key to denominational growth in the past has been the denominational ability to gain agenda harmony for the health and multiplication of local churches. When local churches come together and lock arms, they are able to do what no church can do separately.

NCS has begun working with some synods in the Evangelical Lutheran Church of America. We are finding the same principles apply with the ELCA that also apply to the SBC, United Methodist, Nazarene, Wesleyan, Evangelical Friends, Independent Christian Churches, and others. The structure may be different, but wherever the church is healthy, it is the result of churches gaining agenda harmony and doing together what no local church can do alone.

7. **People from different denominational families can walk hand in hand without seeing eye to eye.** A key person on our NCS team is Phil Spry, founder of TellStart. We come from very different theological backgrounds, but under the NCS umbrella we work together helping launch healthy churches in numbers of different denominational families.

When I think of my friendship with Phil, I am reminded of the Old Testament story of Jehu and Jehonadab, two very different leaders. "Jehu greeted him and said, 'Are you in accord with me, as I am with you?' 'I am,' Jehonadab answered.

'If so,' said Jehu, 'give me your hand.' So he did" (2 Kings 10:15).

To be "in accord" means we extend our hand of fellowship to everyone following the Savior. They may not be part of our denomination, but our Lord taught clearly, "whoever is not against you is for you" (Luke 9:50). I had a pastor write to me when he found out I was working with people beyond my theological tradition. He was concerned and thought we should consider only working with Wesleyan groups. Here in part was the reply I sent to him.

Many of our current NCS Partners are within the Wesleyan tradition. But the NCS Board of Directors has determined that in the spirit of John Wesley, we should serve wherever God gives us opportunities. John Wesley said to George Whitfield when they were at theological odds, "Is your heart one with my heart? Then give me your hand" (2 Kings 10:15-16). As the Lord opens doors for NCS to work—wherever judicatories desire renewal, ReFocusing, church planting, and Parent training—if their hearts are right, we will join hands with them. We believe we can walk hand in hand with numbers of different denominational groups without seeing eye to eye on every issue. Billy Graham has set us a tremendous example in this way, and we hope to follow his spirit and attitude.

◆ ◆ ◆

Churches must refocus their activities, rekindle their spirit, and keep taking risks just like their forefathers did!

◆ ◆ ◆

8. **Denominational families remain strong when they find ways to regularly review how God has worked in their history.** The people of Israel had a way of reviewing their corporate memory and the activity of God among them. One example

was the Israelite crossing of the Jordan River as they entered the Promised Land. Joshua commanded each tribe to set up a stone to remember how God had worked a miracle in the crossing (Josh. 4:4-9).

John Dawson writes, "It is a dangerous thing to lose the knowledge of the past. One of the greatest needs of the church is a sense of her history and destiny."[11] After the people of God entered the Promised Land, established their land, properties, and families, a very tragic thing occurred. It is the same thing that occurs to every denominational family that establishes itself but does not find ways to self-renew. What happens is that the next generation does not experience "the spirit" and sacrifice that shaped the denomination's founding. The people of the denomination no longer grow up in tents; they grow up in buildings. They do not experience the laboring and sacrificing. They only experience enjoying the labor and sacrifice of a previous generation.

The solution to this organizational and spiritual phenomenon is for judicatories to regularly review God's activity. They must renew their structures, refocus their activities, rekindle their spirit, and keep taking risks just like their forefathers did. The Israelites did not experience this renewal and so after the first generation died, "another generation grew up, who knew neither the LORD nor what he had done for Israel" (Judg. 2:10).

Israel's experience is a warning to the church, the new Israel of God. All these things in Israelite history "occurred as examples to keep us from setting our hearts" on the wrong things (1 Cor. 10:6). As a layperson, remember to review the activity of God. The lesson is clear—never forget the days of the tents!

9. **Sectarian attitudes that have caused denominational families to be highly critical of one another are slowly being cleansed out of the church.** All denominational families have great strengths and face similar problems. If you grew up in a

typical denominational climate, chances are good you were taught that your denominational family was *very* right and all the other "tribes" in God's church were *very* wrong. You probably heard some say the chances were good that many people from the other tribes might not even make it to heaven. This sectarian attitude created great zeal to get people to join the right "tribe." The words of Paul are instructive, "I can testify about them that they are zealous for God, but their zeal is not based on knowledge" (Rom. 10:2). Thank God, much of that sectarian, critical spirit is dying away among denominational families.

◆ ◆ ◆

Denominations provide a great history, multiple benefits, and enormous spiritual opportunities to their members.

◆ ◆ ◆

I am not advocating that we erase denominational distinctives, blur theological emphases, or downplay church heritage. I have a number of good friends outside my Wesleyan theological heritage who disagree strongly with me on certain issues. The Scriptures are clear: "There is one body and one Spirit . . . one Lord, one faith, one baptism; one God and Father of all" (Eph. 4:4-6). There is and should be incredible diversity within the broader church of Jesus Christ.

What we should contend for is unity of spirit, without expecting uniformity of practice or belief. It takes all kinds of churches to reach all kinds of people. People who attend New Church University come from a variety of theological backgrounds, but when they all get in a room and begin sharing, they realize they all face the same challenges, grapple with similar issues, and they like each other!

♦ ♦ ♦

Denominations are not just the work of people. Though imperfect, they have been raised up to do the work of God; they are holy and should be treated with reverence and respect.

♦ ♦ ♦

10. **Jesus is present in very imperfect local churches, judicatories, and denominational families.** In the Book of Revelation, we see the resurrected and ascended Christ reappear to the apostle John on the island of Patmos more than 50 years after Pentecost. While the church had spread and grown, there were numbers of churches far from perfect. In detail, Jesus tells John what to write to them. Here you may find one or more things you can identify with regarding the church you attend.

The encouraging thing, despite their problems and challenges, Jesus still walks in the middle of the church! Many are working hard. Some of them may have "forsaken [their] first love" (Rev. 2:4). Some people may be "afraid of what [they] are about to suffer" (v. 10). Some are morally not where they should be (v. 21). Some are in a state of spiritual deadness and need to "wake up" (3:1-2). Some seem to be tired (v. 8) or are spiritually lukewarm (vv. 15-16). With all these problems, what an incredible comfort to know Jesus is still among us. Be encouraged! He is here and walking in the middle of your church!

11. **Denominations provide a great history, multiple benefits, and enormous spiritual opportunities to their members.** My father is a highly committed Christian and loyal member of a denominational family. He is not a pastor. Before retirement, he was a very successful executive manager in a large corporation. I will never forget a conversation we had back in 1989, when I was grappling with what I perceived to be the

imperfections of our denominational family. I can still hear him talking to me in love as he detailed a list of all the benefits and opportunities our family unit had and was receiving because we were an active part of a denominational family.

Twenty Benefits of Denominational Families

Denominations are not just the work of people. Even though imperfect, they have been raised up to do the work of God; they are holy and should be treated with reverence and respect. What follows are some things about spiritual legacy that I can still hear my father teaching me. Because I am in full-time ministry, I have added some of my own learning from across the years.

1. It was the church that came to our community and led your grandparents to Christ.
2. It was the church that created the opportunity for your mother and me to meet when we were teenagers.
3. It was the church that led both of us to Christ and nurtured our faith.
4. It was in the church that we were married and committed our home to God.
5. It was into the church that you were born and given back to God when you were young.
6. It was the church that provided and created the climate that led you to Christ.
7. It was the church that provided religious instruction and training for you during your childhood.
8. It was the church that provided youth activities and opportunities for you during adolescence to stay spiritually connected while facing temptation and secular pressures.
9. It was the church that sponsored and provided a Christian college for you to attend.

♦ ♦ ♦

When you leave or retire from the places you have
served, it will be the church that provides continuity
in ministry transitions, so that your lifetime
of work will not be lost but conserved.

♦ ♦ ♦

10. It was the church that, through its college connection,
    provided you with the Christian life companion you
    have.
11. It was the church that created the atmosphere that ul-
    timately led to your call from God into full-time
    Christian ministry.
12. It was the church that, in your beginning days, gave
    you opportunities to exercise your call to preach.
13. It was the church that provided you with theological
    education.
14. It was the church that provided spiritual accountabili-
    ty, licensed you, and ultimately ordained you into the
    Christian ministry.
15. It was the church that assessed you as a church planter
    and gave you a place to serve.
16. It is the church that continues to provide you with the
    moral and spiritual accountability the Bible teaches
    every minister must have.
17. It is the church that, through your schooling and
    places of service, provides you a rich set of lifelong re-
    lationships with friends and colleagues in ministry.
18. It is the church that allows you to freely participate in
    her government and voice your concerns at the appro-
    priate time.

◆ ◆ ◆

After my father finished and I had prayed, I knew
very clearly what God wanted me to do in my
relationship with my denominational family.

◆ ◆ ◆

19. It is the church that continues to change and adjust
    her ministry to meet the needs of the world, and if you
    are patient, you will see God changing her as He has
    continued to do so for the past 2,000 years.
20. When you leave or retire from the places you have
    served, it will be the church that provides continuity in
    ministry transitions, so that your lifetime of work will
    not be lost but conserved.

After my father finished and I had reflected and prayed, I
knew very clearly what God wanted me to do in my relationship with my denominational family.

You Can Build a Delightful Inheritance

Most of us are the children and grandchildren of some
great people of faith. Whatever your denominational roots,
you have great men and women of faith in your tradition. We
cannot divorce ourselves from our roots or heritage. It is important for us to biblically understand that the lives of the
people preceding us were not just lived on earth. They are a
great cloud of witnesses praying for and encouraging us even
today! (Heb. 12:1).

As I reflect on this truth, let me share how it became personal for me. It requires me to take you back to Kurtz, Indiana. I have stood on the hill where my grandfather is buried
outside of Kurtz. His grave happens to be less than 500 yards
from where the accident occurred that caused his death in
1953. The cemetery is on top of the hill, adjacent to the farm

where he lived and worked. From that hilltop you can look down over the whole valley. You can see the white-frame church and the steeple rising above the houses as the town's tallest building. It is a beautiful country sight.

I never met my grandfather, but I vividly remember standing by his grave and thinking about the spiritual legacy he left me. As I looked across the valley and saw the church from that hill, I could almost sense him standing beside me, with his hand on my shoulder, looking out across the valley as well. As a layperson, he had spent literally thousands of hours traveling across that valley inviting people to church and to a relationship with Christ.

♦ ♦ ♦

"The boundary lines have fallen for me in pleasant places; surely I have a delightful inheritance" (Ps. 16:6).

♦ ♦ ♦

If he could have spoken to me from heaven, I know exactly what he would have said. "Larry, this is what I gave my life for. I gave my life for the church. In doing this, I was following the example of Jesus. Love God with all your heart. Be faithful with all your soul. Stay close to God's Word and let it continue to correct you. Most importantly, love the church!"

You may be reading this and thinking, "I do not have that kind of spiritual heritage." My word to you is, today you can begin building one for yourself, your family, and all the generations that follow you. The testimony of David is my testimony, and it can become yours as well: "The boundary lines have fallen for me in pleasant places; surely I have a delightful inheritance" (Ps. 16:6).

6
A ·
WORLDWIDE
VISION · AND
COMMITMENT

"As the time approached for him to be taken up to heaven, Jesus resolutely set out for Jerusalem" (Luke 9:51, emphasis added).

ALL KINDS OF DIVERSIONS CAME UP along the way for our Lord as He traveled to Jerusalem, headed toward the Cross. When Jesus laid out His mission, which included suffering and death, Peter "took him aside and began to rebuke him. 'Never, Lord!' he said. 'This shall never happen to you!'" (Matt. 16:22). Jesus was severe in His response. "Get behind me, Satan! You are a stumbling block to me; you do not have in mind the things of God, but the things of men" (v. 23). Jesus refused to be distracted.

♦ ♦ ♦

Love for the church is the heart of God. It is also what links us with the hearts of other men and women who are within the church.

♦ ♦ ♦

An ancient adage says, "If you want to defeat them . . . distract them." All during His ministry, Jesus had numerous opportunities to lose His focus. These opportunities usually related to the talents and skills Jesus had. With His power and ability, Jesus could have done many things differently. He could have healed a lot more sick people, taken the time to write some incredible books, or traveled much more widely. But Jesus did not choose any of these options. He was resolute and focused, and through His obedience to the Father, He was powerfully effective.

Loving the Church—Worldwide

What is the spirit that surrounds your life as a Christian? More important than any "specialty" we may have, any competence in our area of expertise, is the spirit that surrounds our lives. What is the atmosphere that people sense when they talk to you? Every person gives attention, consciously or unconsciously, to some kind of vision, which then creates an atmosphere.

We believe the spirit and atmosphere that makes a church healthy, that makes my attitude match that of Jesus, is my spirit of love for the church. This spirit of love must ooze out of us all the time. It is the heart of God. It is also what links us with the hearts of other men and women who are within the church. As Christians, we must be challenged to love the church and give ourselves up for her, just like Jesus did, so that she may be presented to Him without spot or wrinkle, but holy and blameless (see Eph. 5:25-27).

Our love for the church must be as broad as that of Jesus—it must be worldwide. Paul describes the new church in Thessalonica, "The Lord's message rang out from you not only in Macedonia and Achaia—your faith in God *has become known everywhere*" (1 Thess. 1:8, emphasis added). What a tremendous testimony about the spirit of this new church! What would happen if this became the personal commitment of every church? No local church is ever called to build its own kingdom. Jesus taught us to pray, "your kingdom come, your will be done" (Matt. 6:10). Every Christian is called to be a global Christian by Christ (28:19). Your commitment to help develop your local congregation into a worldwide, globally focused church is also the clear vision of the New Testament.

The vision of God in the Old Testament was to use Israel to bring salvation to the entire world. Numerous scripture passages teach this.[12] Jesus' vision for His disciples was worldwide. He clearly has a global vision for every Christian and every congregation today. He challenges us, "Go and make disciples of all nations" (28:19). This is not a mandate just for denominational mission agencies. This is our mission, directly from Jesus himself, given as a mandate to every Christian and every local church. As you and I seek God's vision, we must make sure it is both biblical and global. To be the first (biblical), it must be the second (global).

♦ ♦ ♦

Our attitude toward the global vision of Christ is not just a monetary one, it is a theological one. It is directly linked to our doctrine of ecclesiology.

♦ ♦ ♦

We have seen over and over again that a biblical and global church vision always begins in the heart and attitude of the pastor and laypersons like you. As biblical Christians, our thinking must be the same as that of our Lord—with global objectives always in mind. With Jesus Christ as our leader, God's plan includes our entire planet, and one day it will happen. "The kingdom of the world has become the kingdom of our Lord and of his Christ, and he will reign for ever and ever" (Rev. 11:15). Because this is God's plan for the world, there is a global mission for every church.

When Should World Mission Support Begin?

In many new and existing churches across North America, however, the question is often raised, "Why should we support our denominational missions' efforts? We need money for our ministry here at home. We are not strong enough to give money away. Now is not the time to be concerned about the global call of Christianity. We will be committed to that in the future, just not now."

This is a common attitude found these days throughout the church. It is not a new attitude. This kind of thinking has been around for a long time. I want to suggest that this issue is not just a monetary one, it is a theological one. It again comes down to our basic beliefs about the church. Our answer is directly related to our doctrine of ecclesiology. What do we believe about the nature, mission, and vision of Christ's church?

♦ ♦ ♦

If the DNA for building global Christians is not put into a Christian or local church from day one, we are building a church that is in disobedience to the mission of Jesus.

♦ ♦ ♦

What does Jesus think about this issue? Does He address it in the Scriptures? No serious Christian questions whether or not we should be committed to reaching the entire world with the good news of the gospel. In the Great Commission, our Lord makes very clear, "Go and make disciples of all nations" (Matt. 28:19). The question is, *When* does our mission become global? When does Jesus expect us to be committed globally? In the second year, the fourth year, or the sixth year after we come to Christ?

When does Jesus expect *our church* to be committed to being a globally minded church? When should we make a commitment to begin building global Christians? In the second year, the fourth year, or the sixth year after our church is started? I want to suggest that if the DNA for building global Christians is not put into a Christian from day one, or is not put into a local church from day one, we are discipling a Christian and building a church that is in disobedience to the mission and vision of Jesus.

This is not to say that we expect people who are spiritually less than six months old to be fully committed and take their two-week vacation to go on mission trips. What we are talking about here is the DNA of the church's vision and the heart of the church's laypeople.

Becoming a Global Christian

If I truly seek to have the heart of Jesus, I will seek to think the way He thinks, not just about myself and my ministry, but about the world. I will seek to feel what He feels, to cry over what He cries over, to laugh about what He laughs about, to see what He sees, every day I live. I will not just sing songs in worship services about honoring Him in all I do. I will seek to prove my faith with action (James 2:18).

◆ ◆ ◆

Becoming a global Christian will cause me to wake up every day and think about the world.

◆ ◆ ◆

This will call me to wake up every day and think about the world. All too often the world is out of our vision as Christians; we do not regularly think about it. God sees the world, He thinks about the world, 24 hours a day, seven days a week.

As global Christians, we should too. What follows is a listing of both countries and world areas, organized into nine regions to remind you of the world Jesus loves. We encourage you to take a moment and read the name of each country of the world out loud.

North America (2)

Canada

United States of America

Mexico and Central America (8)

Belize

Costa Rica

El Salvador

Guatemala

Honduras

Mexico

Nicaragua

Panama

Caribbean (24)

Anguilla

Antigua & Barbuda

Aruba

The Bahamas

Barbados

Bermuda

British Virgin Islands

Cayman Islands

Cuba

Dominica

Dominican Republic

French West Indies

Grenada

Haiti

Jamaica

Montserrat

Netherlands Antilles

Puerto Rico (U.S.)

Trinidad and Tobago

Turks and Calcos

St. Kitts and Nevis

St. Lucia

St. Vincent and the Grenadines

Virgin Islands (U.S.)

South America (13)

Argentina

Bolivia

Brazil

Chile

Colombia

Ecuador

French Guiana

Guyana

Paraguay

Peru

Suriname

Uruguay

Venezuela

Africa (52)

Algeria

Angola

Liberia

Libya

Azores
Benin
Botswana
Burkina Faso
Burundi
Cameroon
Cape Verde Islands
Central African Republic
Chad
Comoros
Congo (Brazzaville)
Congo (Kinshasa)
Côte d'Ivoire (Ivory Coast)
Djibouti
Equatorial Guinea
Eritrea
Ethiopia
Gabon
The Gambia
Ghana
Guinea
Guinea—Bissau
Kenya
Lesotho

Madagascar
Mali
Malawi
Mauritania
Morocco
Mozambique
Namibia
Niger
Nigeria
Rwanda
São Tomé and Príncipe
Senegal
Seychelles
Sierra Leone
Somalia
South Africa
Sudan
Swaziland
Tanzania
Togo
Tunisia
Uganda
Zambia
Zimbabwe

Europe (38)

Albania
Andorra
Austria

Belgium
Bosnia and Herzegovina
Bulgaria
Croatia
Czech Republic
Denmark, Greenland, and
    the Faroe Islands
Estonia
Finland
France

Lithuania
Luxembourg
Macedonia
    (former Yugoslav Republic)
Malta
Moldova
Monaco
Netherlands
Norway
Poland

Portugal
Romania
Serbia and Montenegro

Germany
Greece
Hungary
Iceland
Ireland
Italy
Latvia

Slovak Republic
Slovenia
Spain
Sweden
Switzerland and Liechtenstein
Ukraine
United Kingdom and Gibraltar

Middle East (16)

Bahrain
Cyprus
Egypt
Iran
Iraq
Israel, the West Bank, and Gaza
Jordan
Kuwait

Lebanon
Oman
Qatar
Saudi Arabia
Syria
Turkey
United Arab Emirates
Yemen

Central Asia (21)

Afghanistan
Armenia
Azerbaijan
Bangladesh
Belarus
Bhutan
Burma (Myanmar)
Georgia
India
Kazakhstan
Kyrgyz Republic (Kyrgyzstan)

Maldives
Mauritius
Mongolia
Nepal
Pakistan
Russia
Sri Lanka
Tajikistan
Turkmenistan
Uzbekistan

East Asia and Oceania (33)

Australia
Brunei (island of Borneo)
Cambodia
China
East Timor
Fiji
French Polynesia (Tahiti)
Hong Kong
Indonesia

New Caledonia
New Zealand
North Korea
Palau
Papua New Guinea
Philippines
Samoa
Singapore
Solomon Islands

Japan	South Korea
Kiribati	Taiwan
Laos	Thailand
Macau	Tonga
Malaysia	Tuvalu
Marshall Islands	Vanuatu
Micronesia	Vietnam
Nauru	

We encourage you to study the world, become familiar with it, think and pray about it, and ask God to give you a heart for reaching it with the gospel. Depending on how we count territories and dependencies of other nations, there are approximately 206 countries and world areas. God has an incredible desire to extend His love to every one of the 6.5 billion persons who live in them. "God so loved **the world** that he gave his one and only Son" (John 3:16, emphasis added).

If the World Were 100 People

Sometimes the idea of understanding these 6.5 billion people in the world can be a bit overwhelming for some people. It may be easier for us to understand the analogy of the world as a village of 100 people. If that were the case, the following would be a fairly accurate description of it:

- ◆ 61 would be Asian
- ◆ 13 would be African
- ◆ 12 would be European
- ◆ 8 would be South American
- ◆ 6 would be North American
- ◆ 30 would be children and 70 would be adults
- ◆ 52 would be women and 48 would be men
- ◆ 1 would have AIDS
- ◆ 17 would speak Chinese, 9 would speak English, 8 would speak Hindi, 6 would speak Spanish, and 60 would speak something else

- 20 would be undernourished and 1 dying of starvation
- 1 would have a college education, 2 would have a computer, 4 would have access to the Internet, and 14 would be unable to read or write
- 6 people would own 59 percent of the world's wealth, and they would all live in the United States
- the poorest 20 people would share 2 percent of the wealth
- 20 people would live in fear of attack, rape, bombardment, or land mines
- 33 would be Christian
- 19 would be Muslim
- 13 would be Hindu
- 6 would be Buddhist
- 5 would worship spirits in the trees, rocks, rivers, etc.
- 24 would worship something else or nothing

♦ ♦ ♦

Most denominational families have developed a significant group of people who are truly global Christians. We need literally millions more just like them.

♦ ♦ ♦

Most denominational families have developed a significant group of people who are truly global Christians. They see what Jesus sees, consistently. They have reordered their lives accordingly. The challenge we face is that we need literally millions more just like them. We need every pastor to be a global Christian. We need every layperson to get and keep the big picture of the world. Because we follow Christ, our mission is worldwide from the first day we come to Christ and the first day we begin participating in His church.

Embracing a Worldwide Vision

We can only achieve our global objectives as Christians if we keep planting strong, healthy new churches. They must be planted in every country of the world. Churches that are planted in affluent areas must understand Paul's clear teaching on giving (2 Cor. 8—9) and God's concern for the poor. Jesus was born poor, identified with the poor, and ministered to them.[13] Most North American church plants are very wealthy compared to the rest of the world. Getting involved in inner-city ministries and participating in mission trips to developing countries are two ways we can more clearly see the world and its needs from God's perspective.

◆ ◆ ◆

When we as Christians lock arms together in agenda harmony and share a worldwide vision, we have our Lord's promise that then "the world will know!"

◆ ◆ ◆

What is it that you think about every day? What atmosphere surrounds you? What has captured your heart? Where do you invest most of your time and money? I hope God will use this book as a reminder for you to more regularly think the way He thinks about the world and the way He thinks about the church. The world will never believe unless they hear, and they will never hear unless someone preaches to them, and this preaching will not happen unless someone is trained and sent (Rom. 10:14-15).

The vision from heaven for you and me and every other Christian is the same. God calls us to a worldwide commitment. As Christians, we cannot be disobedient to His vision (Acts 26:19). Within your denomination, will you commit today to be part of the sending team about whom the Scriptures speak, "How beautiful are the feet of those who bring good news"? (Rom. 10:15). When we as Christians lock arms together in agenda harmony and share a worldwide vision, we have our Lord's promise that then "the world will know!" (see John 17:23).

NCS MISSION AND MINISTRY DESCRIPTION

Mission: "To assist the starting and strengthening of New-Start, ReStart, ReFocusing, and Parent churches worldwide."

Ministry Description: "New Church Specialties is a nonprofit organization specializing in coaching pastors and church planters, consulting judicatories and denominations, and providing NewStart, ReStart, ReFocusing, and Parent church education and training through New Church University. We exist to serve the mission and ministry of the church."

ABOUT THE AUTHOR

Dr. Larry McKain is the founder and executive director of New Church Specialties, a nonprofit organization currently with a paid staff of 23 and six offices across the United States. He has written the curriculum and launched a training and coaching system for church leaders called New Church University, which has also been translated into Spanish. In the past five years, he has spoken to over 30,000 people and trained 2,600 church leaders through New Church University.

He is a graduate of MidAmerica Nazarene University, Nazarene Theological Seminary, and has an earned doctorate from Fuller Seminary. He has personally planted four churches and has coached and influenced the starting of hundreds of new churches across the U.S. and Canada. His "Insights" e-mail goes out to 7,700 church leaders each week. To date, New Church Specialties has served a total of 19 different denominations.

Larry and his wife, Denise, are the parents of two children, Sarah and Wesley. The McKains make their home in Kansas City.

Contact Information:
    NCS on the Web: www.NewChurchSpecialties.org
    NCS Main Office: Kansas City
    New Church Specialties
    6502 N.W. Mil-Mar Dr.
    Kansas City, MO 64151
    Phone: 816-746-6468
    Fax: 816-746-6444
    E-mail: KCOffice@NewChurchSpecialties.org

NOTES AND CREDITS

1. While we often refer to the church and the kingdom of God interchangeably, they are uniquely different. The church is referred to in the New Testament as a divine-human creation of God, the incarnation of Jesus today, and is an organized community of faith. (See *God, Man, and Salvation*, 597-623.)

2. The church of Jesus Christ is much too complex, diverse, and expansive for us to seek an organized, structural unity. By spiritual unity we mean the focus of Christian activity should not emphasize the differences among denominational families, but rather emphasize our common mission in introducing people to Jesus and making disciples who follow Him throughout the world. We believe this can be done without blurring denominational distinctives or heritage. Unity can be achieved without uniformity.

3. Taken from Charles R. Swindoll, *The Bride* (Grand Rapids: Zondervan Corporation, 1994 by Charles R. Swindoll), 9. Used by permission.

4. W. T. Purkiser, Richard S. Taylor, and Willard H. Taylor, *God, Man, and Salvation: A Biblical Theology* (Kansas City: Beacon Hill Press of Kansas City, 1977), 565.

5. Taken from Rick Warren, *The Purpose-Driven® Church* (Grand Rapids: Zondervan Corporation, 1995 by Rick Warren), 17. Used by permission.

6. Taken from Jim Cymbala, *Fresh Wind, Fresh Fire* (Grand Rapids: Zondervan Corporation, 1997 by Jim Cymbala), 121. Used by permission.

7. The church is a sacramental community, where Christ comes into the presence of a people (see *God, Man, and Salvation*, 575-96). The scope of this book does not allow us to address this issue in depth, but we hope many will want to study further on the subject.

8. Purkiser, Taylor, and Taylor, *God, Man, and Salvation*, 564.

9. Bill Sullivan, *Churches Starting Churches* (Kansas City: Nazarene Publishing House, 2001), 8.

10. Stephen R. Covey, *The Seven Habits of Highly Effective People* (New York: Simon and Schuster, 1989), 9.

11. John Dawson, *Taking Your Cities for God* (Lake Mary, Fla.: Creation House Publishers, 1989), 91.

12. Gen. 12:3; Ps. 2:8; 19:4; 22:27; 65:5; 67:7; 98:2-3; Isa. 45:22; 49:6; 52:10; Jon. 4:11; Mic. 5:4 is just a beginning sample of scriptures.

13. Many passages explain God's heart for the poor and weak: Ps. 41:1; Prov. 19:17; Isa. 10:1-2; Amos 8:4-7; Luke 4:18-19; 7:20-23; James 1:27. The New Testament reveals that many early Christians were poor and God expected the church to treat them properly (1 Cor. 1:26-29; James 2:1-9).